Fabulous Beans

by Barb Bloomfield

The Book Publishing Company
Summertown, Tennessee

Cover and interior design by Barbara McNew
Cover photo by John Guider
Back cover photo by Valerie Epstein

Copyright © 1994 Barb Bloomfield

Pictured on the front cover: Pasta Bean Salad, page 35.

99 98 97 96 95 94   1 2 3 4 5 6 7 8 9

The Book Publishing Company
P.O. Box 99
Summertown, TN 38483

ISBN 0-913990-17-5
Bloomfield, Barb, 1950-
    Fabulous beans / Barb Bloomfield.
                p.   cm.
    Includes index.
    ISBN 0-913990-17-5
    1. Cookery (Beans) 2. Vegetarian cookery. I. Title.
TX803.B4B58   1994
641.6'565--dc20   94-18045
                                                   CIP

Calculations for the nutritional analysis in this book are based on the average number of servings listed with the recipes and the average amount of an ingredient if a range is called for. Calculations are rounded up to the nearest gram. If two options for an ingredient are listed, the first one is used. Not included are optional ingredients, serving suggestions, or fat used for frying, unless the amount of fat is specified in the recipe.

Dedicated to
My Mom
*who showed me that
creativity and good nutrition in the kitchen
make a strong family.*

TABLE OF CONTENTS

Introduction 8
    Cooking Beans.. 9
    Preparing Beans... 9
    Freezing Beans 10
    Bean Cooking Chart 11
    Types of Beans 12

Dips and Spreads 15
    White Bean Spread 15
    Gremalata.. 16
    DARK STAR Dip 16
    Garbanzo Spread 17
    Hummus... 18
    Hummus-Eggplant Dip 18
    West Indies Bean Dip 19
    Barbecue Black Bean Dip 20
    Lentil Pâté 21
    Carrot-Garbanzo Dip 22
    Golden Yellow Split Pea Dip 23
    Soy Nuts... 24
    Chick-Pea Nuts 24

Salads 25
    Carrot and Garbanzo Salad 25
    Lima Gazpacho Salad 26
    Tabouli.. 27
    Kidney Bean and Sprouted Lentil Salad 28
    Tropical Black Bean Salad 29
    Taco Salad 30
    Lentil-Lime Salad 31
    Pineapple-Lentil Salad....................................... 32
    Kidney Bean Salad 33
    White Bean Salad 34
    Pasta Bean Salad 35
    Crunchy Soybean Salad 36

Thai Style Bean Salad.............................37
Olive Pasta Salad 38
Sweet 'n Sour Cabbage-Kidney Salad 39

Soups.. 40

Autumn White Bean Soup 40
African Split Pea Soup 41
Great Northern Mushroom Soup 42
Yellow Split Pea Soup 43
Mixed Bean and Noodle Soup 44
Black Bean Soup 45
Creamy Pinto Soup 46
Pasta Plus Soup................................47
Sprouted Lentil Soup 48
Hearty Bean 'n Grain Soup 49
Summer Minestrone Soup 50
Lentil Soup with Greens 51
Triple Bean Soup 52
Creamy Corn Soup..............................53
Split Pea Soup..................................54
Spicy Golden Soup 55
Composite Soup................................56
White Bean Chowder 57
Karhi and Pakoris 58

Main Dishes.................................... 60

Pat's Baked Beans 60
Noodle-Veggie-Bean Casserole 61
Moussaka 62
Spicy Pinto Casserole 64
Melted Yeast Cheeze Sauce 65
Enchiladas....................................66
Mexican Corn Bean Pie 68
Lentil Loaf 70
Garbanzo-Vegetable Loaf 71
Island Loaf 72

5

Stuffed Acorn Squash 73
Stuffed Cabbage with Black-Eyed Peas 74
Soy Stuffed Peppers 76
Tamale Stuffed Peppers 77
Black Eyed Spirals 78
Eggplant Rolls 80
Bean Sausage Links 81
Falafel 82
Pinto Burgers 83
Lentil Burgers 84
Soy Burgers 85
Pinto Pies 86
Meatless Pinto Balls 87
Curried Veggie Fritters 88
Autumn Stew 89
Lentil-Vegetable Biryani 90
Spanish Stew 91
White Bean and Squash Stew 92
Kidney-Polenta Stew 93
Lentil Stew 94
Kidney-Yam Stew 95
Garbanzo-Sweet Potato Stew 96
Easy White Bean Stew 97
Lentils 'n Barley 98
Sweet 'n Sour Garbanzo Medley 99
Barbecue Soybeans 100
Lentils and Eggplant 101
Tanzanian Kidneys with Coconut 102
Spicy Lentils 103
Sweet and Sour Soybeans 104
Garbanzo Gumbo 105
Curried Garbanzos 106
Bean Sprout Curry 107
Sprouted Lentils 108
Garam Masala 108

Soybean Stroganoff 109
Armenian Beans 110
Curried Limas 111
Summer Lentils and Veggies 112
Ceci all' Italiana 113
Black-Eyed Peas with Greens 114
Brazilian Black Beans 115
Lima Combo over Couscous 116
Fruity Beans 117
Marinara Lentil Sauce 118
Diane's Eggplant and Black-Eyed Pea Curry 119
Coccari's Masoor Dal 120
Soybeans in Sweet Sauce 121
Anasazi Beans in Miso Sauce 122
Spanish Yellow Split Peas 123
Split Pea Curry 124
Butternut Aduki Skillet 125
Orange-Ginger Garbanzos 126
Caribbean Black-Eyed Pea Stir-Fry 127
East Indian Kidneys 128
Anasazi Beans and Rice 129
Lentils and Rice 130
Hoppin' John 131
White Bean Tzimmis 132
Spicy Anasazi Beans 133
Black Beans and Noodles 134
Pasta Fagioli 135
Bean Balls with Mushroom Gravy 136
Succotash 137

Desserts 138
Tutti-Fruity Bars 138
Aduki Carob Cake 139
Sweet Bean Pie 140

Index 141

Introducing the fabulous bean!

Introduction

We do our bodies and the earth such a favor by eating beans. I hope you will become familiar with the various types of beans, the methods for preparing them, and the diverse range of recipes you can use to enjoy them, so that beans can be a common part of your diet. How can we ignore one of the oldest foods known to humankind? Archeologist have unearthed fossilized lentils from periods prior to 8000 BC. All cultures use beans in their traditional dishes. Beans are the only cultivated food plants that improve the fertility of the soil they are grown in through the beneficial bacteria which live on their roots and bring nitrogen from the air into the soil. Eating beans has overwhelming benefits for our health. High in protein, carbohydrates, fiber, and B vitamins and low in fat and sodium, beans also contain significant amounts of calcium, iron, and potassium. Research has repeatedly shown that eating beans contributes to lowering cholesterol (LDL) and blood pressure levels which helps prevents clogged arteries and heart disease. Beans produce a slow rise in blood sugar, which is important for people with diabetes. It has been shown that both breast cancer and colon cancer can be controlled by hormone-like substances which are activated by digestive inhibitors in beans. Beans help in the regulation of the colon, preventing constipation and hemorrhoids.

What about gas that is so often associated with eating beans? Humans lack the enzyme alpha-galactosidase which is needed to digest the complex sugars in beans. When these sugars are attacked by bacteria in our lower intestines gas is the result. The more frequently you eat beans, the easier it is to digest them. Go easy on the portions; over eating beans is asking for trouble. If you pre-soak your beans, strain off the soaking water, discard it, and cook them in fresh water; it will help reduce gas. The water the beans are cooked in still makes a rich bean stock. (I always save this stock and use it later in soups, bread, biscuits, or gravy.) You can also add a 4" strip of kombu, a sea vegetable, which aids in digestion, to your pot of beans. You can also try

Beano®, the liquid form of alpha-galactosidase. A few drops on your first bite of beans alleviates gas. *Allergy Note:* Beano® is made from a safe food grade mold, however very rarely a sensitivity with allergic-type symptoms, can occur. If this happens to you, discontinue using the product; if you know you are *galactosemic*, consult your doctor before trying it.

Preparing Beans

Before soaking or cooking beans, check them for pieces of dirt, stones, twigs, or other foreign matter that needs removing. Rinse them in a colander while rubbing the beans through your hands to clean them. It isn't necessary to pre-soak beans (especially if you're going to pressure cook them), but it does cut down on the cooking time. Soak beans in three times as much water as beans, either overnight or the morning before you're going to cook them for supper. You can also use the quick-soak method. After you have checked the beans, rinse them, put them in a covered pot, and bring them to a boil for one minute. Keep them covered and soak for 1 hour. This will plump the beans up just like soaking overnight. Change the water and you are ready to cook the beans. Refer to the cooking chart on page 11 to find the right cooking times. You can cook most beans in an open kettle or in a pressure cooker.

Cooking Beans

Most of my recipes call for cooked beans; the cooking of the beans isn't listed as part of the recipe. If you're pressed for time and need to open a can, go ahead. Please be aware that many brands of canned beans have salt, sugar or corn syrup, and preservatives added, so rinse them before adding to a recipe.

Store your dry beans in airtight containers in a cool, dark, dry place. I do, however, keep larger amounts of our most often used beans in bags, and I have never had insects get into them.

Cooking and Freezing the fabulous bean!

If you look over the recommended times for cooking beans from one cookbook to the next, you might see quite a range of opinion on how long is long enough. Commercially canned beans are not as soft as the beans you might cook at home, but for most people, canned beans won't cause digestive problems. But because there are enough people whose systems don't do well with beans unless they are cooked *very soft* (especially children and elderly people), I recommend cooking times for beans that may seem more than necessary to you. Until you are sure that the people you are cooking for can handle a tougher bean, cook your beans until you can easily mash them on the roof of your mouth with your tongue. You shouldn't have to chew them to get them to break up easily. The cooking times listed on the chart on page 11 will provide you a with good guideline for cooking various types of beans until they are soft enough even for young children.

Cooking beans in a microwave isn't a time saver if you're starting with dry beans. Of course, if the beans are already cooked, they heat up fine, but I've found using a microwave to cook dry beans doesn't decrease the cooking time significantly over top-of-the-stove methods.

Crock pots or slow cookers are a convenient way to prepare beans. Before you leave the house in the morning, put in a cup or two of rinsed beans, three times as much water, some garlic, a bay leaf perhaps, and turn to a low setting. Your beans will be ready to use for an evening meal. Soybeans won't cook sufficiently with this method; use a pressure cooker instead.

Freezing Beans

When cooking beans, try to cook a full pot at a time and freeze the leftovers for future meals. Beans freeze well. You can store them in pint or quart containers in your freezer and have them ready to use without having to cook them each time. Defrost them in the morning before using them that night. If you want to freeze beans to put into a salad, drain the cooked beans, spread them out on a cookie sheet, and freeze. When they are frozen, put them in an airtight container. This is a good idea for summer picnics; they'll help keep your cooler cold while they defrost. Bean soups and stews freeze well too, so make a full pot and freeze some for when you don't have time to prepare a meal.

When referring to the cooking chart, remember that cooking times will vary depending upon how old the beans are. Older beans take longer to cook than fresher ones that have more moisture in them. Apply the cooking times referred to here after the water has come to a boil and been turned down to a simmer (for open kettle) or come up to pressure (for pressure cooking). Also keep in mind that your altitude may effect the cooking times. At altitudes higher than sea level you may need to add several minutes on to these times.

Bean Cooking Chart

Use three cups of water for each cup of dried beans.

	Soaked, open-kettle	No soak and pressure cook	Soak and pressure cook	Yield per 2 cups dry
aduki	30 min	15 min	5-10 min	6 ⅔
anasazi	60 min	25 min	15 min	5
black	90 min	30-35 min	20 min	5
black-eyed peas	25 min	10 min	5-8 min	4 ¾
garbanzo	4 hr. 25 min	35 min	25 min	5
Great Northern	90 min	25 min	20 min	5
kidney	35-40 min	30 min	15-20 min	4 ½
lentil, brown*	20-25 min	**	**	5
lentil, orange*	15-20 min	**	**	3 ⅓
lima, baby	30 min	10-15 min	8 min	4
navy	35-40 min	22 min	15 min	5
pinto	90 min	35-40 min	20-25 min	5
soybeans	**	60 min	45 min	4
split peas*	75-90 min	7 min	**	4

* It is not necessary to presoak lentils and split peas.
**Do not use this method for this variety of beans.

11

Types of fabulous beans!

Types Of Beans

From the many kinds of beans that exist, I have chosen the most available ones to use in my recipes. If you able to find others to work with, don't hesitate to substitute them.

Aduki beans (adzuki)—These small Asian beans are easy to digest and sweet in flavor. They cook quickly so watch closely to prevent them from getting mushy. If you cook them with rice, they turn the rice a pretty shade of pink. You may have to go to an Asian or natural food store to find these beans, and they are more expensive than domestic beans, but they're worth the price.

Anasazi beans—The ancestor of pinto beans, these lovely purple and white flecked beans have a rich flavor. Anasazi means "ancient ones" in the Navaho language. Anasazi beans cook faster than pintos and go well in Mexican dishes with chile peppers, garlic, and cumin.

Black beans (turtle)—Black beans are a staple of Cuban, Latin American, and Asian diets. They are low in fat and go well with corn and rice. Think of using coriander and lime juice for spicing up your black beans.

Black-eyed peas (cowpeas)—These thin skinned peas are popular in recipes from India, Africa, and the southeastern United States. They cook quickly and make great stuffings, casseroles, and soups. Black-eyed peas have a distinct, nutty flavor and are low in fat and high in iron.

Garbanzo beans (chick-peas)—You'll find these round, beige beans in dishes from the Mediterranean and India. They are a good source of calcium, and have the highest fat content of all beans, except soybeans. Their nutty flavor makes them very versatile. Try them in dips, soup, salads, curries, or burgers.

Great Northern beans—See White beans

Kidney beans—Kidney beans have a distinct, rich flavor, a firm texture, and are a good source of iron and potassium. They make the best chili but also are good in salads, soups, and casseroles.

Lentils (pulses, dal)—Lentils, derived from Latin "lens" are perhaps the oldest legume of our civilization. There are many kinds of lentils: green, brown, and orange are the ones most commonly found in this country. Lentils are easy to sprout. They cook quickly, have a creamy texture, and are great in curry dishes.

Lima beans (baby limas and butter/large)—Lima beans originated in South America. A starchy bean, they have more potassium and vitamin C than any other legume. When soaked, limas cook quickly; watch them carefully if you want to use them in a salad and keep their shape .

Navy beans—See White beans

Pinto beans—The popular pinto bean . . . plump, with pinkish brown flecks and earthy flavor that goes so well with Mexican spices: garlic, chillies, and cumin. Pinto cultivation is abundant in southwest Colorado, although the beans are native to Mexico.

Types of fabulous beans!

Soybeans—From central China we get the nutritious and versatile soybean. It contains all of the essential amino acids, lecithin, and has the highest fat content of any legume. The list of soy based foods is impressive: tofu, tempeh, soy sauce, textured vegetable protein, soy oil, soy flour and grits, soymilk, soy ice cream, soy yogurt, and miso. I recommend adding a teaspoon of oil to the pressure cooker before cooking soybeans. They tend to foam up, and their hulls will clog the vents. Keep an ear out when cooking them - if the steady sizzle of steam is interrupted you should turn off the heat, bring down the pressure, and check to see that the vent is not clogged. Cleaning up a pressure cooker explosion is no fun.

Split peas—Besides the common green split pea, you'll also find the yellow variety which has a milder flavor. Good for soups and dips, split peas are a good source of vitamin A and are very low in fat. It's not necessary to presoak split peas. They take a little over an hour to cook in an open kettle.

White beans (Navy, Great Northern) —We all know these beans as baked beans but they're also good for soups and stews. They don't take long to cook. Compared with other beans they're high in fiber, calcium, and vitamin E. The mild flavor of these beans goes well with thyme, savory, or rosemary.

Dips and
*   *
# Spreads

White Bean Spread

Yields 2 ¼ cups
You can eat this spread with pita bread, crackers, or raw vegetables.

2 cups cooked white beans (navy or lima), mashed

Drain and mash the cooked beans.

½ cup tomatoes, finely chopped
¼ cup red onions, minced
½ tsp cumin
¼ tsp salt
⅛ tsp black pepper
juice of 1 lemon

While the beans are hot, add the tomatoes, onions, cumin, salt, black pepper, and lemon juice, and mix well.

May be served warm or cold.

Per ¼ cup: Calories: 59, Protein: 3 gm., Fat: 0 gm., Carbohydrates: 11 gm.

Gremalata

Yields 2 cups

This is a tasty dip that can be served with raw carrots and peppers or on crackers or rice cakes.

10 cloves garlic, peeled

Roast the peeled garlic in the oven for 10 minutes at 350°.

2 cups cooked white beans (navy or lima)
¼ cup fresh lemon juice
¼ cup fresh parsley, chopped
½ tsp salt
¼ tsp black pepper

Combine the roasted garlic together with the beans, lemon juice, parsley, salt, and black pepper in a blender. Add a little bean stock if the dip seems too thick.

Per ¼ cup: Calories: 70, Protein: 4 gm., Fat: 0 gm., Carbohydrates: 13 gm.

DARK STAR Dip

Yields 4 cups

My son created this recipe and consumes massive quantities of it when we have taco salad for dinner.

3 cups pinto beans
⅓ cup onions, chopped
⅓ cup green peppers, chopped
½ cup tomatoes, chopped
½ cup spaghetti sauce
½ cup mild or hot salsa
1 jalapeño pepper
½ tsp salt

Blend all of the ingredients together in a food processor, but leave the dip somewhat chunky.

Per ¼ cup: Calories: 53, Protein: 3 gm., Fat: 0 gm., Carbohydrates: 10 gm.

Garbanzo Spread

Yields 3 ½ cups

Enjoy this spread with a chunk of Italian or dark rye bread.

½ tsp olive oil
1 clove garlic, chopped
½ cup onions, chopped

Sauté the onions and garlic in the olive oil until soft.

½ cup fresh parsley, chopped
1 Tbsp fresh basil, chopped,
    or 1 tsp dried basil
1 tsp fresh oregano, or ½ tsp dried
    oregano

Add the herbs to the onions and garlic, and continue to sauté just until the parsley leaves have softened.

¼ tsp cumin
2 Tbsp fresh lemon juice
3 cups cooked garbanzo beans, mashed
½ cup bean stock
½ tsp salt

Mix all of the ingredients together with a fork, or puree in a food processor.

Per ¼ cup: Calories: 62, Protein: 3 gm., Fat: 0 gm., Carbohydrates: 10 gm.

Hummus

Yields 2 cups

This is a rich spread that goes well on pita bread with sprouts and tomato. We like it as a travel food to put in our cooler when we can't prepare a meal.

2 cups cooked garbanzo beans
¼ cup bean stock
¼ cup lemon juice
2 cloves garlic
1 Tbsp soy sauce
3 Tbsp tahini
2 Tbsp fresh parsley, chopped

Puree all of the ingredients together, and let them sit for at least 30 minutes before eating to let the flavors develop.

Per ¼ cup: Calories: 106, Protein: 4 gm., Fat: 4 gm., Carbohydrates: 14 gm.

Hummus-Eggplant Dip

1 small eggplant

Bake the eggplant at 350° for 20-30 minutes until it is soft in the middle. Scoop out the soft inside, and mash well. Add to the hummus dip.

Per ¼ cup: Calories: 125, Protein: 4 gm., Fat: 4 gm., Carbohydrates: 18 gm.

West Indies Bean Dip

Yields 2⅔ cups

Here's a spicy dip that is good to serve with corn chips as an appetizer or party snack.

2½ cups cooked pinto or kidney beans
¼ cup onions, finely chopped
1 tomato, chopped (about ⅔ cup)
1 Tbsp soy sauce
2 Tbsp lemon or lime juice
¼ cup bean stock
½ tsp curry powder
½ tsp oregano
½ tsp chili powder
1 tsp coriander
1 tsp cumin
2 cloves garlic, minced

Blend all of the ingredients together in a food processor, or mash the beans with a fork, and mix well with all of the other ingredients.

Per ¼ cup: Calories: 64, Protein: 3 gm., Fat: 0 gm., Carbohydrates: 12 gm.

Barbecue Black Bean Dip

Yields 2 ¼ cups

¾ cup onions, chopped
½ tsp canola oil

2 cups cooked black beans
4 Tbsp tomato paste
¼ cup vinegar
2-3 Tbsp honey or brown sugar
1 Tbsp vegetarian Worcestershire
**   sauce**
1 Tbsp mustard
½ tsp allspice
salt to taste

Sauté the onions in the canola oil until they begin to brown.

Combine all of the ingredients in a food processor, and process until you have a smooth dip.

Serve with corn chips or celery sticks.

Per ¼ cup: Calories: 87, Protein: 3 gm., Fat: 0 gm., Carbohydrates: 17 gm.

Lentil Pâté

Yields 3 cups

You may slice this thin to serve with crackers, or keep it in a block that can be dipped into or spread with a knife.

3 cups water
1 cup dried lentils

In a medium saucepan, bring the water and lentils to a boil, lower the heat, cover, and cook for 30-35 minutes.

2 cups sourdough bread

Break up or chop the sourdough bread, and place in a medium bowl. When the lentils have finished cooking, pour any extra cooking water into a measuring cup. Press the lentils with the back of a slotted spoon to allow the extra stock to flow into the cup. Add enough water to make 1 cup of liquid, and pour it over the sourdough bread pieces. Stir to soften all of the bread.

1 cup celery (3 stalks), chopped
1 cup onions, chopped
1 tsp olive oil

In a skillet, sauté the celery and onions in the olive oil until soft.

2 Tbsp soy sauce
1 tsp tarragon
1 tsp thyme
¼ tsp ground cloves
⅛ tsp black pepper

Preheat the oven to 350°.
In a food processor, combine the drained lentils, soaked bread, onions and celery, soy sauce, tarragon, thyme, cloves, and black pepper, and blend together until well mixed. Pour this mixture into a lightly oiled bread pan, and bake for 40 minutes. Cool and refrigerate overnight. The pâté will slip out of the pan when it is turned over onto a serving plate.

Per 2 tablespoons: Calories: 38, Protein: 2 gm., Fat: 0 gm., Carbohydrates: 6 gm.

Carrot-Garbanzo Dip

Yields 3 cups

1 cup bean stock or water
2 cups carrots, cut into ½" chunks
2 cloves garlic, coarsely chopped
⅔ cup onions, chopped

1 ½ cups cooked garbanzo beans,
        drained
2 tsp dried mint
2 Tbsp lemon juice
½ tsp salt

In a medium saucepan, bring the stock or water, carrots, garlic, and onions to a boil. Lower the heat and simmer for 10-15 minutes.

Combine all of the ingredients in a food processor until smooth. Place in a serving bowl, and serve with toasted pita bread pieces, rice cakes, or raw pepper and celery sticks.

Per ¼ cup: Calories: 49, Protein: 2 gm., Fat: 0 gm., Carbohydrates: 9 gm.

Golden Yellow Split Pea Dip

Yields 2 cups

1 cup yellow split peas
3 cups water

In a medium saucepan, bring the water and yellow split peas to a boil, lower the heat, cover, and simmer for 1¼ hours or until the peas are quite soft. Stir occasionally while simmering.

2 Tbsp orange juice concentrate
2 cloves garlic, minced (1 Tbsp)
2 Tbsp white miso
½ tsp paprika
2 Tbsp nutritional yeast

After the split peas have cooked, cover and let stand until they are cool; then drain off any excess liquid. In a food processor, mix the orange juice concentrate, garlic, miso, paprika, yeast, and split peas, and puree until smooth.

Per ¼ cup: Calories: 80, Protein: 5 gm., Fat: 0 gm., Carbohydrates: 14 gm.

Soy Nuts

Yields 3 cups

These crunchy, roasted beans are a great snack. They are high in protein but not as high in fat as regular nuts. Take them with you hiking, or have them on hand for afternoon snacks.

2 cups dried soybeans
4 cups water

Soak the soybeans in the water overnight. The next morning, drain off the soak water, and add enough fresh water to cover the beans one inch. Bring to a boil for 5 minutes, and remove any hulls that float to the top. Cover the beans and let them stand for an hour or longer.

Preheat the oven to 350°. Drain the beans and pour onto a lightly oiled cookie sheet. Spread the beans out into a single layer, and bake for 35-45 minutes until lightly browned. Shake the pan or stir with a wide spoon or spatula a few times during the baking. Remove the soybeans from the oven, and sprinkle with salt. Let the beans cool completely, and store them in an air tight container; they keep well.

Per ¼ cup: Calories: 78, Protein: 7 gm., Fat: 3 gm., Carbohydrates: 7 gm.

Chick-Pea Nuts

Prepare as for *Soy Nuts*, but use chick-peas instead of soybeans. For Spiced Chick-Pea Nuts sprinkle the beans with soy sauce and garlic powder before baking.

Per ¼ cup: Calories: 45, Protein: 2 gm., Fat: 0 gm., Carbohydrates: 8 gm.

* Salads *

Carrot and Garbanzo Salad

Serves 4-6

Prepare this salad ahead of time, and let it marinate for the full flavor to develop.

*2 cups cooked garbanzo beans
   [1 (15 oz.) can]
1 cup carrots, grated
1 cup cucumbers, grated
1 clove garlic, pressed
2 scallions, finely chopped
¼ cup fresh parsley, minced*

Combine the beans, carrots, cucumbers, garlic, scallions, and parsley in a medium serving bowl.

*2 Tbsp tahini
1 Tbsp water or apple juice
1 Tbsp balsamic vinegar
1 tsp soy sauce*

To prepare the dressing, combine the tahini, water or apple juice, vinegar, and soy sauce in a small jar with a tight fitting lid, and shake vigorously until well mixed. Pour the dressing over the salad, mix, and refrigerate a few hours before serving, if possible. Stir a few times while the salad is sitting.

Per serving: Calories: 166, Protein: 6 gm., Fat: 5 gm., Carbohydrates: 24 gm.

Lima Gazpacho Salad

Serves 6

This salad is better if it is made ahead of time and is allowed to marinate for a few hours before serving. Consider this as an accompaniment to a picnic or cook-out.

2 cloves garlic, minced
5 scallions, chopped
1 green pepper, chopped
1 cucumber, chopped
2 cups fresh tomatoes, chopped
1 avocado, chopped
2 cups cooked lima beans, chilled

Mix the garlic, scallions, green pepper, cucumber, tomatoes, and avocado in a bowl, and gently stir in the cold lima beans.

1 Tbsp olive oil
¼ cup balsamic vinegar
¼ tsp basil
¼ tsp oregano
salt and pepper to taste

To prepare the dressing, combine the olive oil, vinegar, basil, oregano, salt, and pepper in a small jar with a tight fitting lid, and shake vigorously until well mixed. Pour the dressing over the salad, mix thoroughly, and chill until ready to serve.

Per serving: Calories: 179, Protein: 6 gm., Fat: 6 gm., Carbohydrates: 24 gm.

Tabouli

Serves 6

The addition of garbanzo beans to the this traditional dish makes a complete meal.

2 cups water
1 cup bulgur

Bring the water to a boil in a small saucepan. Remove the pan from the heat, add the bulgur, mix well, and cover tightly. Let stand for 30 minutes, allowing to cool completely before adding to salad.

½ cup fresh peppermint
2 cloves garlic
2 Tbsp soy sauce
¼ tsp black pepper
2 Tbsp olive oil
⅓ cup fresh lemon juice

To prepare the dressing, combine the peppermint, garlic, soy sauce, black pepper, olive oil, and lemon juice in a blender.

1 cup fresh parsley, chopped
½ cup green onions, chopped
2 large tomatoes, chopped
cucumber
½ cup ripe olives, pitted and chopped in halves (optional)
1½ cups cooked garbanzo beans, chilled

In a salad bowl, combine the parsley, green onions, tomatoes, cucumber, olives, and garbanzo beans with the bulgur. Pour the dressing over the salad, toss well, and chill for several hours before serving.

Per serving: Calories: 227, Protein: 8 gm., Fat: 5 gm., Carbohydrates: 36 gm.

Kidney Bean and Sprouted Lentil Salad

Serves 6

¼ cup apple cider
1 Tbsp olive oil
3 Tbsp wine vinegar
2 Tbsp soy sauce
¼ tsp black pepper
½ tsp paprika
2 Tbsp fresh dill weed, minced,
   or 1 tsp dried dill

1½ cups cooked kidney beans
1½ cups cooked green beans
¾ cup Sprouted Lentils (see page 108)
1½ cups cooked rice
1 cup celery
⅔ cup red onions, sliced
1 cup bell pepper, chopped

To prepare the dressing, mix the apple cider, olive oil, wine vinegar, soy sauce, black pepper, paprika, and dill weed in small jar with a tight fitting lid, and shake vigorously until well mixed.

In a salad bowl, combine the beans, lentils, rice, celery, onions, and bell pepper, pour the dressing over all, and mix until well blended. It's good to chill the salad to allow the flavors to develop before serving.

Per serving: Calories: 178, Protein: 7 gm., Fat: 2 gm., Carbohydrates: 32 gm.

Tropical Black Bean Salad

Serves 6

Thanks to Rose who gave me the idea for this one. These may seem like unusual ingredients to combine, but it makes a unique salad or entree. Try serving it with fresh corn bread or a dark loaf of pumpernickel.

3 cups cooked black beans, cooled
½ cup onions, chopped
3 cloves garlic, minced
1 jalapeño pepper, minced
3 Tbsp fresh lime juice
2 cups mangos, cubed (2-3 fruits)
2 cups fresh pineapple, chopped
½ tsp salt

In a medium serving bowl, combine all of the ingredients, stir gently, and serve, or refrigerate overnight to marinate.

Per serving: Calories: 182, Protein: 7 gm., Fat: 0 gm., Carbohydrates: 36 gm.

Taco Salad

Serves 5

This is a fun meal because everyone gets to make unique combination to suit their tastes. Amounts to have on hand will vary depending on the appetite of those eating.

**1 (12 oz.) package fat-free corn chips
3 cups cooked pinto beans,
mashed, or 2-3 cups DARK
STAR Dip (see page 16)**

Toppings:
**1 carrot, grated
1 onion, chopped
1 green pepper, chopped
1 cucumber, chopped
1 tomato, chopped
1 avocado, thinly sliced (optional)
2 cups lettuce, finely chopped,
        or alfalfa sprouts**

Condiments:
**hot salsa
mayonnaise
ketchup
mustard
nutritional yeast**

To assemble, crush a handful of corn chips on a plate, spoon on some mashed beans or bean dip, and sprinkle on any or all of the toppings, followed by the condiments of your choice.

Per serving: Calories: 280, Protein: 11 gm., Fat: 2 gm., Carbohydrates: 53 gm.

Lentil-Lime Salad

Serves 4-6

1 ½ cups lentils
1 bay leaf
1 clove garlic, cut into chunks
5 cups water

In a saucepan, bring the lentils, bay leaf, garlic, and water to a boil. Lower the heat, cover, and cook 25-30 minutes until the lentils are soft. Remove the bay leaf and garlic, drain, and cool.

3 scallions, finely chopped
½ cup celery, chopped
¼ cup fresh parsley, minced
½ fresh chili pepper, minced

In a medium serving bowl, combine the drained lentils with the scallions, celery, parsley, and chili pepper.

2 Tbsp soy sauce
1 Tbsp red wine vinegar
3 Tbsp lime juice
1 Tbsp olive oil
2 cloves garlic, minced or pressed
½ tsp grated lime peel
½ tsp cumin

To prepare the dressing, combine the soy sauce, vinegar, lime juice, olive oil, garlic, lime peel, and cumin in a small jar with a tight fitting lid, and shake vigorously until well mixed. Pour the dressing over the lentil/vegetable mixture, mix gently, and refrigerate for at least an hour to enhance the flavors.

Per serving: Calories: 174, Protein: 10 gm., Fat: 2 gm., Carbohydrates: 27 gm.

Pineapple-Lentil Salad

Serves 6

1 tsp olive oil
1 tsp cumin
½ tsp coriander
2 tsp gingerroot, grated

In a medium skillet, heat the olive oil and add the cumin, coriander, and gingerroot. Stir constantly until the spices begin to release a pleasant aroma.

2 ½ cups cooked lentils, drained

Add the lentils, mix with the spices, remove from the heat, and cool.

1 (20 oz.) can unsweetened pineapple
     chunks, (save the juice)
2 large tomatoes, chopped

In a serving bowl, combine the pineapple chunks, tomatoes, and lentils.

2 Tbsp apple cider vinegar
1 Tbsp soy sauce
1 tsp spicy mustard
1 clove garlic, minced
⅓ cup pineapple juice
     (reserved from chunks)

To prepare the dressing, combine the vinegar, soy sauce, mustard, garlic, and pineapple juice in a small jar with a tight fitting lid, and shake vigorously until well mixed. Pour the dressing over the bowl of pineapple, tomatoes, and lentils, and toss well. Chill before serving.

Per serving: Calories: 172, Protein: 7 gm., Fat: 1 gm., Carbohydrates: 32 gm.

Kidney Bean Salad

Serves 6
Basmati rice is good for this salad.

2 cups cooked kidney beans
2 cups cooked rice
1 bell pepper, chopped
⅓ cup raisins
⅓ cup walnuts, chopped
3 scallions, chopped

Combine the beans, rice, bell pepper, raisins, walnuts, and scallions in a serving bowl.

juice of 1 lemon
1 cup soy yogurt
1 clove garlic
1 Tbsp honey
1 tsp coriander
½ tsp turmeric
1 tsp cumin
½ tsp Garam Masala (see page 108)
½ tsp salt

To prepare the dressing, combine the lemon juice, yogurt, garlic, honey, coriander, turmeric, cumin, garam masala, and salt in a blender. Pour the dressing over the salad, and mix well.

Per serving: Calories: 244, Protein: 8 gm., Fat: 5 gm., Carbohydrates: 42 gm.

White Bean Salad

Serves 4-6

3 ½ cups cooked white beans, drained
3 cloves garlic, minced
6-8 scallions, chopped
½ cup black olives, chopped (optional)
½ cup fresh parsley, chopped
¼ cup fresh mint, chopped,
**   or 1 tsp dried mint**
1 Tbsp olive oil
1 Tbsp apple cider
1 tsp salt
¼ tsp thyme
¼ tsp tarragon
¼ cup lemon juice
¼ tsp black pepper

Combine all of the ingredients in a mixing bowl, and refrigerate for several hours or overnight before serving.

Per serving: Calories: 205, Protein: 11 gm., Fat: 2 gm., Carbohydrates: 34 gm.

Pasta Bean Salad

Serves 6

1 ½ cups dried pasta (small shells, spirals, or elbows)

Cook the pasta al dente, drain, and cool.

2 cups broccoli, chopped into bite-sized spears
½ cup carrots, cut into match sticks

Blanch the broccoli and carrots for 3 minutes; drain, rinse with cold water, and set aside.

½ cup scallions, sliced
1 bell pepper, chopped
2 cups cooked pinto beans, chilled
¼ cup fresh parsley, chopped

Combine the pasta, broccoli, carrots, scallions, bell pepper, pinto beans, and parsley in a salad bowl.

¼ cup lemon juice
2 cloves garlic, minced
2 Tbsp soy sauce
1 Tbsp olive oil
2 Tbsp water or apple juice
1 tsp crushed basil

To prepare the dressing, combine the lemon juice, garlic, soy sauce, olive oil, water or apple juice, and basil. Blend the dressing ingredients in a blender, or place in a jar with a tight fitting lid, and shake vigorously until well mixed. Toss the salad with the dressing, and serve.

Per serving: Calories: 224, Protein: 9 gm., Fat: 3 gm., Carbohydrates: 40 gm.

(Pictured on the cover.)

Crunchy Soybean Salad

Serves 6

1 bunch scallions, chopped
2 carrots, shredded
2 stalks celery, finely chopped
1 cup mung bean sprouts
*2 cups Chinese cabbage, finely
    chopped*
½ cup water chestnuts, sliced
1 Tbsp toasted sesame seeds
2 cups cooked soybeans

1 Tbsp olive oil
2 Tbsp wine vinegar
2 Tbsp soy sauce
¼ cup apple juice
1 clove garlic, minced
1 Tbsp gingerroot, grated
1 chili pepper, finely chopped

In a medium salad bowl, combine the scallions, carrots, celery, sprouts, cabbage, water chestnuts, sesame seeds, and soybeans, pour on the dressing, and mix well. Chill and stir occasionally before serving.

To prepare the dressing, combine the olive oil, vinegar, soy sauce, apple juice, garlic, gingerroot, and chili pepper in a small jar with a tight fitting lid, and shake vigorously until well mixed.

Per serving: Calories: 141, Protein: 8 gm., Fat: 6 gm., Carbohydrates: 14 gm.

Thai Style Bean Salad

Serves 6

A tangy dressing brings this combination of beans alive.

3 cups green beans, cut diagonally

Cook the green beans until crisp-tender. Cool with cold water.

2 cups cooked white beans or lima beans

Cook the white beans until they are soft but not mushy.

2 cloves garlic, minced
½ cup lime juice
3 Tbsp soy sauce
1 Tbsp sugar
¼ tsp salt
1 fresh chile or jalapeño pepper, seeded and thinly chopped
½ cup fresh mint leaves, minced

To prepare the dressing, combine the garlic, lime juice, soy sauce, sugar, salt, chile pepper, and mint in a jar with a tight fitting lid, and shake vigorously until well mixed.

Combine the green beans and white beans in a serving bowl, and pour the dressing over the beans, mixing carefully so the beans stay whole. Refrigerate at least an hour before serving.

Per serving: Calories: 119, Protein: 7 gm., Fat: 0 gm., Carbohydrates: 23 gm.

Olive Pasta Salad

Serves 6

3 ½ cups cooked pasta spirals
     (2 cups dry)
2 ½ cups cooked garbanzo beans
1 ½ cups celery, chopped
¾ cup scallions, chopped
1 cup salad olives

In a salad bowl, combine the pasta, garbanzo beans, celery, scallions, and olives.

1 Tbsp olive oil
¼ cup red wine vinegar
¼ cup water or apple cider
1 Tbsp soy sauce
1 Tbsp honey
1 tsp spicy mustard
½ tsp paprika

To prepare the dressing, combine the olive oil, vinegar, water or apple cider, soy sauce, honey, mustard, and paprika in a blender, or mix them together in a jar with a tight fitting lid, and shake vigorously until well mixed. Pour the dressing over the pasta, and mix well. Serve or refrigerate, stirring occasionally, until ready to serve.

Per serving: Calories: 250, Protein: 9 gm., Fat: 5 gm., Carbohydrates: 42 gm.

Sweet 'n Sour Cabbage-Kidney Salad

Serves 6

1 cup broccoli, chopped

Steam the broccoli for 3 minutes; drain, and cool immediately.

½ cup celery, chopped
1 cucumber, thinly sliced
1 cup cabbage, shredded
2 cups cooked kidney beans

Place the broccoli, celery, cucumber, cabbage, and kidney beans in a salad bowl.

3 Tbsp soy sauce
3 Tbsp cider vinegar
1 Tbsp honey
1 Tbsp olive oil
1 clove garlic, minced

To prepare the dressing, combine the soy sauce, vinegar, honey, olive oil, and garlic in a small jar with a tight fitting lid, and shake vigorously until well mixed. Pour the dressing over the salad, mix, and refrigerate for several hours, stirring occasionally.

Per serving: Calories: 126, Protein: 6 gm., Fat: 2 gm., Carbohydrates: 20 gm.

* Soups *

Autumn White Bean Soup

Serves 4

This soup can be made quickly with precooked beans, or you can start with one cup of dry beans, cook them for an hour in your stock, and then proceed with the directions.

5 cups stock or water
5 scallions (¼ cup), finely chopped
2 cloves garlic, minced
1 cup turnips, chopped small
⅓ cup millet

In a soup pot, bring the stock or water to a boil, and add the scallions, garlic, turnips, and millet; cover and cook for 15 minutes.

1 cup fresh, frozen, or canned green
       beans, chopped
½ cup mushrooms, sliced
2 cups cooked white beans
       (navy, Great Northern, etc.)
¼ cup parsley, chopped
2 Tbsp soy sauce
½ tsp tarragon
¼ tsp rosemary

Add the green beans, mushrooms, white beans, parsley, soy sauce, tarragon, and rosemary to the soup, and continue to cook for 10 minutes. Turn off the heat, keep covered, and let the soup sit for 5 minutes before serving. Add more water if it is too thick.

Per serving: Calories: 253, Protein: 12 gm., Fat: 1 gm., Carbohydrates: 48 gm.

African Split Pea Soup

Serves 4

Be ready for an exotic treat when you embellish the plain split pea with this array of spices.

4 whole cloves
4 peppercorns
1 stick cinnamon

1 ½ cups dried split peas
5 cups water
1½ cups onions, chopped
1 cup tomato, chopped
1 chili pepper, minced
½ tsp ginger powder
½ tsp garlic powder
½ tsp cardamom
1 tsp turmeric
2 tsp coriander
2 tsp cumin
½ tsp chili powder

Tie the cloves, peppercorns, and cinnamon stick in a piece of cheesecloth so they can be removed later.

In a heavy soup pot, combine all of the ingredients, and bring to a boil. Lower to a simmer, and cook, partially covered, for 1½ hours. The split peas should become soft and begin to disintegrate. Remove the peppercorns, cloves, and cinnamon stick before serving. Add salt to taste after the soup has cooked.

Per serving: Calories: 200, Protein: 11 gm., Fat: 0 gm., Carbohydrates: 37 gm.

Great Northern Mushroom Soup

Serves 4

This creamy soup with chunks of vegetables is mellow and soothing, perfect for a weekend lunch. I hope you can find some unusual mushrooms to vary the flavor of this soup from time to time.

1 cup dried Great Northern beans, or 2½ cups canned Great Northern beans
4 cups water

If you are starting with dried beans, in a medium soup pot, cook the beans in the water until soft, about 1¼ hours.

2 cups mushrooms, sliced
1 medium onion, chopped
1 clove garlic, minced
½ cup carrots, diced small
½ tsp olive oil

In a medium skillet, sauté the mushrooms, onion, garlic, and carrots in the olive oil until soft.

3 cups bean stock or veggie broth
¼ tsp thyme
¼ tsp savory
¼ tsp marjoram
½ tsp salt
⅛ tsp black or white pepper

In a blender or food processor, blend the beans with the stock or broth. Pour the blended beans back into the soup pot, and add the sautéed vegetables, thyme, savory, marjoram, salt, and pepper. Bring to a slow boil, lower heat, and simmer for 5 minutes.

Per serving: Calories: 166, Protein: 9 gm., Fat: 0 gm., Carbohydrates: 30 gm.

Yellow Split Pea Soup

Serves 6

I like to have a batch of muffins or chewy bread on hand to eat with this soup. It lends itself to dunking as you enjoy the subtle mint flavor.

2 cups dry yellow split peas (1 lb.)
8 cups water

1½ cups onions, chopped
1 Tbsp garlic cloves, minced
1 chili pepper, minced (optional)
1 tsp paprika
1 tsp coriander
1 tsp olive oil

2 cups fresh or canned tomatoes,
**   chopped**
2 Tbsp tomato paste

2 Tbsp fresh lemon juice
1 Tbsp fresh mint, chopped,
**   or 1 tsp dried mint**
1 tsp salt

In a heavy soup pot, cook the yellow split peas until soft, about 1 hour.

In a medium skillet, while the yellow split peas are cooking, sauté the onions, garlic, chili pepper, and spices in the olive oil for 3-5 minutes. Stir to prevent sticking.

Add the tomatoes and tomato paste to the skillet of onions and garlic, and simmer for 20 minutes.

When the yellow split peas are soft enough to start falling apart, add the tomato/onion mixture, lemon juice, mint, and salt, bring to a boil, and simmer for 15 minutes.

Per serving: Calories: 201, Protein: 11 gm., Fat: 1 gm., Carbohydrates: 36 gm.

Mixed Bean and Noodle Soup

Serves 4-5

This is a thick soup in which you can use a variety of leftover beans to create the interesting textures and flavors.

1 cup onions, chopped
2 cloves garlic, minced
1 ½ chili peppers, minced,
      or ¼ tsp crushed dry hot
      pepper
1 tsp olive oil

In a soup pot, sauté the onions, garlic, and chili pepper in the olive oil for 3-5 minutes until soft.

¾ cup noodles, small shells,
      or elbow macaroni

Cook the noodles in boiling water for 6 minutes while preparing the rest of the soup. Drain the noodles and set aside.

1 ½ cups tomato puree
2 cups water or bean broth
1 cup cooked white beans
1 cup cooked red kidney beans
1 cup cooked garbanzos beans
1 tsp dried mint
1 tsp dried dill
½ tsp salt

While the noodles are cooking, add the tomato puree, water or broth, beans, and spices to the soup pot, bring to a boil, and lower to a simmer. Add the noodles, and cook for 5 minutes. Serve immediately or the noodles will become overcooked.

Per serving: Calories: 263, Protein: 11 gm., Fat: 2 gm., Carbohydrates: 48 gm.

Black Bean Soup

Serves 6

Eating black beans, dark and warming, is comforting any time of the year. With or without the scoop of rice, corn meal muffins go well with this soup.

1 lb. dry black beans (2 cups)
8 cups water
1 bay leaf
1 large onion, finely chopped
1 green pepper, chopped

Soak the beans overnight; drain and rinse. In a soup pot, combine the soaked beans with the water, bay leaf, onion, and green pepper, and simmer for 1½-2 hours until the beans are very soft.

1 tsp oregano
2 tsp cumin
1 tsp salt
2 Tbsp lemon juice

Add the oregano, cumin, salt, and lemon juice, and cook for 5 more minutes. Serve with a scoop of cooked rice in the middle of each bowl if you wish, and garnish with chopped scallions.

Per serving: Calories: 202, Protein: 11 gm., Fat: 0 gm., Carbohydrates: 37 gm.

Creamy Pinto Soup

Serves 4

You can make this soup as hot as you like by varying the amount and kind of peppers you use. I like to serve a tossed green salad to accompany this soup.

⅔ cup onions, chopped
1 clove garlic, minced
1 chili or jalapeño pepper, minced
½ tsp olive oil

In a medium soup pot, sauté the onions, garlic and pepper in the olive oil for several minutes.

1½ cups fresh or canned tomatoes, chopped
3 cups cooked pinto beans
2 cups bean broth
½ tsp cumin powder
½ tsp oregano
½ tsp salt

Add the tomatoes, beans, bean broth, cumin, oregano, and salt to the pot, bring to a boil, and cook for 10 minutes. In a food processor, puree the soup several cups at a time. Return to the pot, cover, and cook over low heat until ready to serve. Garnish with crumbled corn chips if you wish.

Per serving: Calories: 204, Protein: 10 gm., Fat: 1 gm., Carbohydrates: 38 gm.

Pasta Plus Soup

Serves 6

You'll like this combination of greens, pintos, and noodles. It's a wholesome meal all in one dish, and you can choose which greens and what kind of pasta to use.

3 cloves garlic, minced
1 cup celery, chopped
1 cup onions, chopped
1 tsp olive oil

In a large soup pot, sauté the garlic, celery, and onions in the olive oil.

3 cups cooked pinto beans
3 cups water
3 cups tomato juice
1 lb. (4-5 cups) spinach, kale,
       or collards, chopped

Add the beans, water, tomato juice, and greens to the soup pot, and bring to a boil.

1 cup uncooked pasta, macaroni,
       or small shells
1 tsp salt

Add the pasta and salt, return to a boil, and turn down to a medium heat, stirring occasionally. Cook for 10 minutes, remove from the heat, cover, let sit for 5 minutes, and serve.

Per serving: Calories: 262, Protein: 11 gm., Fat: 2 gm., Carbohydrates: 50 gm.

Sprouted Lentil Soup

Serves 5

Sprouted lentils add a crisp texture to soups that contrasts with the cooked vegetables. The miso in this recipe imparts a rich flavor that enhances the leeks and dill.

½ tsp olive oil
2 cloves garlic, minced

In a medium soup pot, sauté the garlic in the olive oil until browned.

4 cups vegetable broth, bean broth, or water
1 cup leeks, chopped
1 cup carrots, chopped
1 cup potatoes, chopped

Add the broth, leeks, carrots, and potatoes to the pot, and simmer for 15 minutes.

3 cups Sprouted Lentils (see page 108)
1 tsp dried dill,
or 2 Tbsp fresh dill, chopped

Add the lentil sprouts and dill, and bring to boil.

3 Tbsp mugi (dark) miso

Turn the heat off and mix in the miso; cover and let sit for 5 minutes before serving.

Per serving: Calories: 127, Protein: 4 gm., Fat: 1 gm., Carbohydrates: 24 gm.

Hearty Bean 'n Grain Soup

Serves 6

This filling soup is one you'll want to prepare for cold winter evenings to keep you warm. The chewy barley and fragrant rosemary give a distinctive flavor to this soup.

½ *cup barley*
½ *cup bulgur*
½ *cup split peas*
½ *cup lentils*
1 *bay leaf*
1 *onion, chopped*
2 *cloves garlic, chopped*
6 *cups water*

In a medium soup pot, cook the barley, bulgur, split peas, lentils, bay leaf, onion, and garlic in the water for 50 minutes.

1 *cup cooked soybeans,*
    or other cooked beans
2 *cups raw spinach, chopped*
¼ *cup soy sauce*
¼ *tsp rosemary*

Add the soybeans, spinach, soy sauce, and rosemary to the soup pot, and continue cooking for 20 more minutes. Add more water if necessary.

Per serving: Calories: 210, Protein: 13 gm., Fat: 3 gm., Carbohydrates: 33 gm.

Summer Minestrone Soup

Serves 6-8

When garden produce is available, this soup offers a special freshness. How can you resist the deluge of vegetables transformed into this scrumptious soup?

1 Tbsp minced garlic
1 cup onions, finely chopped
1 tsp olive oil

5 cups vegetable stock, bean stock,
    or water
1 cup soaked white beans,
    or 2½ cups cooked white
    beans (add to soup later)
⅓ cup long grain rice
4 cups tomatoes, chopped
1 cup green beans, cut into 1" pieces
1 cup zucchini, cubed
¾ cup carrots, sliced
½ cup celery, chopped
1 cup potatoes, cubed
1 bay leaf
¾ tsp dried sage
¾ tsp rosemary
2 Tbsp fresh basil, chopped
¼ cup fresh parsley, chopped

½ tsp salt
½ cup wine (optional)

In a large soup pot, sauté the onions and garlic in the olive oil, stirring to avoid sticking, until lightly browned.

Add all of the ingredients except the salt and wine to the soup pot, and bring to a gentle boil. If using cooked beans, add to the soup with the salt and wine below. Cover and cook for 1 hour, stirring occasionally.

Add the salt and wine, and simmer for 10 more minutes. Turn off the heat and let sit for 10 minutes before serving.

Per serving: Calories: 177, Protein: 7 gm., Fat: 1 gm., Carbohydrates: 34 gm.

Lentil Soup with Greens

Serves 6

This soup is like a hearty stew. Enjoy it with a chunk of corn bread or crusty Italian bread.

1 ½ cups dried lentils
8 cups water

Rinse the lentils well, then bring to boil in the water. Lower the heat to a simmer, and cook gently for 45 minutes.

1 cup onions, chopped
3 cloves garlic, minced
1 tsp canola oil

Sauté the onions and garlic in the canola oil for 5 minutes.

1 ½ lbs. (6 cups) greens, chopped:
spinach, Swiss chard,
collards, kale etc.
¼ cup parsley, chopped
2 Tbsp tomato paste
½ tsp cumin powder
½ tsp crushed chili peppers
½ tsp salt

Add the onions and garlic, greens, parsley, tomato paste, and spices to the lentils, and stir well. Cook over medium heat for 15 minutes.

Per serving: Calories: 169, Protein: 10 gm., Fat: 1 gm., Carbohydrates: 29 gm.

Triple Bean Soup

Serves 4-6

The fresh parsley and basil give this mixed bean soup a special flavor. Topped with roasted sunflower seeds, this soup is one you'll want to serve again and again.

½ cup pinto beans
½ cup navy beans
½ cup dried lima beans
5 cups water

Soak the beans overnight; drain and rinse, add 5 cups of fresh water, and cook for 1 hour.

1 cup onions, chopped
1 green pepper, chopped
1 cup celery, chopped
1 chili pepper, chopped
1 tsp olive oil

Sauté the onions, green pepper, celery, and chili pepper in the olive oil until soft.

1 Tbsp fresh basil, chopped
⅓ cup fresh parsley, chopped
½ tsp coriander

Add the basil, parsley, coriander, and sautéed vegetables to the beans, and cook about 1 hour until everything is tender.

½ tsp salt
½ cup roasted sunflower seeds, coarsely ground, (optional)

Add the salt and garnish with sunflower seeds before serving.

Per serving: Calories: 98, Protein: 4 gm., Fat: 1 gm., Carbohydrates: 17 gm.

Creamy Corn Soup

Serves 5-6

My kids love this creamy soup with corn and a dash of dill.

3 cups cooked lima beans
3 cups bean broth

Blend the beans and broth in a food processor or blender, and set aside.

¾ cup onions, chopped
1 tsp canola oil
2 cups fresh or frozen corn

In a medium soup pot, sauté the onions in the canola oil until soft, add the corn, and cook until hot.

2 Tbsp flour
2 Tbsp fresh dill, chopped,
**   or 1 tsp dried dill**
½ tsp salt
⅛ tsp black pepper

Stir the flour, dill, salt, and black pepper into the pot of onions and corn.

1 ½ cups soymilk

Add the soymilk gradually and stir until any lumps dissolve. Simmer for 3 minutes, add the bean puree, and heat slowly until hot throughout. Serve immediately.

Per serving: Calories: 222, Protein: 10 gm., Fat: 2 gm., Carbohydrates: 42 gm.

Split Pea Soup

Serves 6

This soup is one of our favorites; as cold leftovers it makes a good spread on bread or crackers.

1 lb. (2 cups) split peas
2 quarts water

Rinse the split peas and add cold water.

1 bay leaf
1 cup onions, chopped
2 cloves garlic, minced
1 cup celery, chopped
2 cups sweet potatoes, cubed
¼ tsp thyme

Add the bay leaf, onions, garlic, celery, sweet potatoes, and thyme to the peas, and cook until the split peas are soft, about 1-1½ hours. Add the salt and pepper to taste.

salt and pepper, to taste

If a smooth, creamy soup is desired, you may puree it in a food processor.

Per serving: Calories: 218, Protein: 10 gm., Fat: 0 gm., Carbohydrates: 43 gm.

Spicy Golden Soup

Serves 4-6

Here is a spicy soup that is good served with a chunk of bread for dipping.

2 cloves garlic, minced
1 onion, chopped
1 tsp canola oil

In a medium soup pot, sauté the garlic and onion in the canola oil until soft.

1 tsp coriander
1 tsp turmeric
½ tsp garam masala (see page 108)
¼ tsp crushed red pepper

Add the spices and cook for several minutes, stirring frequently.

6 cups water
1½ cups dried yellow split peas

Add the water and yellow split peas, bring to a boil, and lower the heat. Cover and simmer for 1½ hours, until the peas begin to loose their form.

½ tsp salt
1 Tbsp lime juice

Add the salt and lime juice just before serving.

Per serving: Calories: 159, Protein: 9 gm., Fat: 1 gm., Carbohydrates: 28 gm.

Composite Soup

Serves 6-8

A composite of beans, grains, and vegetables lets you create a meal in one pot. If you have other vegetables on hand to substitute, try them.

1 cup dried baby lima beans
½ cup yellow split peas
7 cups water

In a large soup pot, bring the lima beans, split peas, and water to a boil; lower the heat, cover, and cook for 35 minutes.

¼ cup barley
¼ cup brown rice

Add the barley and rice, cover, and continue to cook for 25 minutes.

1 onion, chopped
1 potato, cubed
1 cup carrots, chopped
1 cup celery, chopped
2 cups tomato puree or juice
1 cup mushrooms, chopped

Add the onion, potato, carrots, celery, tomato puree, and mushrooms, and simmer for 20 minutes.

¼ cup fresh dill, chopped
¼ cup fresh parsley, chopped
1 tsp salt
¼ tsp black pepper

Add the dill, parsley, salt, and black pepper to the soup, and cook on a low heat for 5 minutes. Let the soup sit with the lid on for a few minutes, and serve hot.

Per serving: Calories: 205, Protein: 8 gm., Fat: 0 gm., Carbohydrates: 42 gm.

White Bean Chowder

Serves 6

There is no need to open a can to enjoy the treat of chowder.

1 cup dried navy beans
4 cups water

Soak the beans in 4 cups of water overnight and drain off the water. Add 3 cups of fresh water, bring to boil, and cook for 30 minutes at a simmer.

¾ cup onions, chopped
2 medium potatoes, cubed
2 carrots, diced
2 stalks celery, diced
1 cup tomatoes, pureed

Add the vegetables to the bean pot, and cook 35 more minutes. Take 3 cups of the bean/vegetable mixture, puree in a food processor or blender, and return it to the simmering soup.

2 cups soymilk
1 Tbsp nutritional yeast
1 tsp salt
⅛ tsp black pepper
2 Tbsp parsley, chopped

Add the soymilk, nutritional yeast, salt, black pepper, and parsley while stirring constantly. Let the soup simmer for a few minutes until it thickens.

Per serving: Calories: 172, Protein: 9 gm., Fat: 1 gm., Carbohydrates: 30 gm.

Karhi and Pakoris

Serves 3-4

This Indian dish, traditionally made with buttermilk, is a thick soup with dumplings that is usually eaten with plain rice. The sour/spicy flavor of this dish is a real treat.

Karhi

⅜ *cup chick-pea flour*

Sift the chick-pea flour into a bowl.

¾ *cup cooked white beans*
½ *cup water*
2 *tsp vinegar*

Combine the beans, water, and vinegar in a blender until smooth, add gradually to the chick-pea flour, and mix well until you have a thick, smooth paste.

2½ *cups water*

Add the water to the bowl of thick bean/flour paste, mix well, and set aside.

1 *tsp canola oil*
⅛ *tsp fennel seeds*
⅛ *tsp cumin seeds*
⅛ *tsp black mustard seeds*
pinch fenugreek seeds

In a heavy-bottomed soup pot, heat the canola oil over medium heat. When it is hot, add the fennel, cumin, black mustard, and fenugreek seeds, and stir while they start to pop.

¼ *tsp crushed red pepper*
½ *tsp turmeric*

When the seeds have darkened, add the red pepper, turmeric, and the bean/flour mixture. Bring to a boil, lower heat, cover, and simmer gently for 1 hour, stirring occasionally.

1-1½ *Tbsp lemon juice*
½ *tsp salt*

Add the lemon juice and salt, cover, and cook 10 more minutes.

Pakoris (dumplings)

These can be made while the karhi is cooking.

½ *cup chick-pea flour*
¼ *tsp baking powder*
¼ *tsp salt*
¼ *tsp ground cumin*
¼ *cup water*

Sift the chick-pea flour, baking powder, salt, and cumin into a bowl. Add the water slowly, mixing as you go, until you have a thick, doughy paste. Heat a skillet or wok over medium heat, put a few drops of oil in the skillet, and spread it with a spatula to cover the bottom. Drop the batter using a teaspoon; use a second spoon to release the paste.

Lower the heat and cook the dumplings slowly, turning a few times to cook evenly. The dumplings should maintain their yellowish color. Don't cook them until they turn brown.

Have a bowl of warm water standing by. When the dumplings are done, lift them into the warm water, and let them soak for 2 minutes. Remove the dumplings from the water, and squeeze them very gently, taking care not to break them. Cover and set aside.

When the karhi is done, lift the cover off the dumplings, and put them in the soup. Just before serving, heat the karhi and pokaris to a simmer. Serve over rice.

Per serving: Calories: 220, Protein: 10 gm., Fat: 2 gm., Carbohydrates: 36 gm.

* Main Dishes *

Pat's Baked Beans

Serves 4

Whip this together and make some potato salad while it's baking. This is a great dish to include in an outdoor meal menu. Be sure the kids are there; they'll love these baked beans.

3 cups cooked navy beans
1 cup bean stock
1 tsp onion powder,
       or 1 small onion, diced
½ tsp garlic powder
1 heaping Tbsp yellow mustard
¼ cup ketchup
⅓ cup molasses
¼ cup brown sugar

Preheat the oven to 300°.
Mix all of the ingredients together, and bake for 45 minutes in a shallow, 2-quart baking dish until thick but not dry.

Per serving: Calories: 336, Protein: 10 gm., Fat: 1 gm., Carbohydrates: 71 gm.

Noodle-Veggie-Bean Casserole

Serves 4-5

Be creative with this dish. Use whatever vegetables you have on hand, or enjoy this variation.

¾ cup onions, chopped
1 cup celery, chopped
1 tsp canola oil

In a medium skillet, sauté the onions and celery in the canola oil until lightly browned.

3 Tbsp whole wheat flour
1½ cups soybean stock

Add the flour to the sautéed onions and celery, stirring well to spread evenly. Stir constantly while adding the bean stock, a little at a time until thoroughly combined. Bring to a boil while stirring until the sauce thickens.

1 carrot, grated
1 cup corn, fresh or frozen
1 tomato, chopped
½ tsp salt
⅛ tsp black pepper
¼ tsp sage
½ tsp tarragon
¼ tsp thyme

Add the carrot, corn, tomato, and spices to the sauce, and simmer for several minutes.

Preheat the oven to 350°.

1 cup cooked soybeans
2 cups cooked whole wheat noodles

In a lightly oiled 3-quart casserole dish, spread the soybeans, noodles, and vegetable sauce.

1 tomato, sliced
¼ cup parsley, minced

Arrange the sliced tomato on top of the casserole, sprinkle with the parsley, and bake for 20-25 minutes.

Per serving: Calories: 228, Protein: 10 gm., Fat: 4 gm., Carbohydrates: 38 gm.

Moussaka

Serves 6

This Greek casserole is a good one to prepare ahead of time. You can store it in the refrigerator, and heat it up when you are ready to serve.

2 medium eggplants
salt

Slice the eggplant into ¼" rounds, sprinkle with salt, and let sit in a bowl while you prepare the filling and white sauce. The salt will draw out some of the bitterness from the eggplant. Rinse the salt off before layering the eggplant in the casserole.

1 cup onions, chopped
2 cloves garlic, minced
1 tsp olive oil

In a medium skillet, sauté the onions and garlic in the olive oil until the onions start to brown.

2 cups tomato puree
2 Tbsp lemon juice
½ tsp cinnamon
½ tsp salt
⅛ tsp pepper
¼ cup parsley, chopped
2 cups cooked garbanzo beans, mashed

Add the tomato puree, lemon juice, spices, parsley, and garbanzo beans to the skillet of sautéed onions and garlic, and cook over low heat, stirring occasionally, for 15 minutes.

Preheat the oven to 350°.

White sauce:
¼ cup unbleached white flour
2 cups low-fat soymilk
½ cup nutritional yeast flakes

In a small saucepan over medium heat, whisk together the flour, soymilk, and nutritional yeast.

1 Tbsp margarine
½ tsp salt

When the sauce thickens, add the margarine and salt, stir well, and cover until ready to use.

**½ cup bread crumbs, for topping
(optional)**

To assemble, layer the rinsed eggplant and half of the bean filling in a lightly oiled 9" x 13" baking pan. Repeat, ending with a layer of eggplant. Pour the white sauce over the entire casserole, sprinkle with bread crumbs if desired, and bake for 35-45 minutes. Cool for 10 minutes before cutting into squares.

Per serving: Calories: 282, Protein: 13 gm., Fat: 5 gm., Carbohydrates: 45 gm.

Spicy Pinto Casserole

Serves 6

1 cup onions, chopped
1 Tbsp garlic, minced
1 hot chili pepper, minced,
    or ¼ tsp dried chili,
    or cayenne
1 tsp canola oil

In a heavy-bottomed soup pot, sauté the onions, garlic, and hot pepper in the canola oil until soft.

1 Tbsp chili powder
1 tsp oregano
1 tsp cumin
3 cups canned or pureed tomatoes
1 cup water

Add the spices, tomatoes, and water to the pot, and bring to a boil.

1 cup uncooked macaroni or shells
½ tsp salt

Add the pasta and salt to the pot, and simmer for 15 minutes.
Preheat the oven to 325°.

1½ cups corn
3 cups cooked pinto beans
½ cup sliced black olives (optional)

Add the corn, pinto beans, and olives to the pasta and tomato mixture, and stir until heated throughout. Spoon this mixture into a 3-quart casserole dish.

1 cup baked corn chips, crushed
1 cup Melted Yeast Cheeze Sauce
    (see page 65)

Top with the corn chips and Cheeze Sauce, and bake for 15-20 minutes until the Cheeze Sauce begins to brown.

Per serving: Calories: 400, Protein: 15 gm., Fat: 2 gm., Carbohydrates: 77 gm.

Melted Yeast Cheeze Sauce

Yields 2 cups

This sauce keeps well in the refrigerator if stored in a tightly sealed container. Use as a cheese spread, on macaroni, or for pizza topping.

2 cups water
2 Tbsp unbleached white flour
2 Tbsp cornstarch
½ cup nutritional yeast flakes
½ tsp salt
½ tsp garlic powder
¼ tsp turmeric (optional)

Mix the water, flour, cornstarch, nutritional yeast, and spices together in a medium saucepan, and cook over medium heat, stirring constantly, until the sauce begins to bubble and thicken. Turn off the heat.

2 tsp prepared mustard
1 Tbsp soy margarine

Add the mustard and margarine while the sauce is still hot. Stir well and cover until ready for use, or cool down and store until later. The sauce will thicken considerably as it cools. It may be re-heated (you may need to add a little water) or used as a spread.

Per ¼ cup: Calories: 53, Protein: 3 gm., Fat: 2 gm., Carbohydrates: 6 gm.

Enchiladas

Serves 6

This is an easy dish to prepare, especially if your beans are already cooked. We like it on cool fall evenings, accompanied by a fresh green salad.

Filling:
1 cup onions, chopped
3 cloves garlic, minced
½ tsp canola oil

In a heavy skillet, sauté the onions and garlic in the canola oil until the onions are soft.

4 cups cooked pinto beans
½ cup bean stock
1 Tbsp tomato paste
2 Tbsp soy sauce
1 tsp cumin

Add the beans, bean stock, tomato paste, soy sauce, and cumin to the skillet, and simmer for 8-10 minutes. Turn off the heat and mash the beans.

Sauce:
½ cup onions, chopped
½ cup green peppers, chopped
1 Tbsp garlic, minced
½ tsp canola oil

While the bean filling is cooking, sauté the onions, green peppers, and garlic in the canola oil in a heavy, 2-quart saucepan.

3 cups tomatoes, pureed
2 cups water
3½ Tbsp chili powder
2 tsp cumin
½ tsp oregano
½ tsp salt

Add the tomatoes, water, and spices to the onions, green peppers, and garlic, and simmer for 10 minutes, stirring occasionally to prevent sticking.

Preheat the oven to 350°.

10 corn tortillas

Lightly oil a 9" x 13" baking dish. Scoop one cup of sauce into the baking dish, and spread it around to cover the bottom. Take a tortilla with a pair of tongs, and dip it into the tomato sauce (this keeps the tortilla from cracking when it is folded over). Place it on an empty plate to assemble. Spoon ⅓ cup of the filling along the center of the tortilla, and wrap it around the bean filling. Place it in the baking dish with the overlapped side down. When all the tortillas are rolled and in the pan, pour the remaining sauce over the top, and bake for 20-25 minutes.

Per serving: Calories: 204, Protein: 10 gm., Fat: 1 gm., Carbohydrates: 37 gm.

Mexican Corn Bean Pie

Serves 6-8

This is a favorite of ours. It's easy to prepare and delicious with a green salad.

2 cloves garlic, minced
¾ cup onions, chopped
1 tsp canola oil

In a medium skillet, sauté the garlic and onions in the canola oil.

1 cup frozen or fresh corn
½ cup green peppers, chopped
1½ cups fresh or canned tomatoes,
**   chopped**

Add the corn, green peppers, tomatoes, and spices to the skillet, and cook 5 minutes, stirring occasionally.

1 tsp cumin
1 Tbsp chili powder

½ cup black olives, chopped
3½ cups cooked pinto beans
**   [2 (15 oz.) cans]**

Add the olives and pinto beans, and heat gently until the topping is ready to assemble.

Preheat the oven to 350°.

Topping:
⅔ cup cornmeal
⅔ cup unbleached white or whole
**   wheat flour**
1 tsp baking powder (+ ½ tsp baking
**   soda if honey is used)**
¼ tsp salt

Stir the cornmeal, flour, baking powder, and salt together in a medium mixing bowl.

¾ cup low fat soymilk
1 Tbsp canola oil
3 Tbsp sugar,
**   or 2 Tbsp honey**

Make a well in the middle of the dry ingredients, and add the soymilk, canola oil, and sweetener. Mix the liquid and dry ingredients enough to combine, but don't beat smooth. Place the corn/bean mixture in an oiled 3 quart casserole dish (about 9" diameter). Spoon over the corn bread topping, smooth it out to cover most of the bean filling, and bake for 35 minutes.

Per serving: Calories: 303, Protein: 10 gm., Fat: 5 gm., Carbohydrates: 54 gm.

Lentil Loaf

Serves 4-6

1 small onion, chopped
1 tsp olive oil

2 cups cooked lentils, drained
½ cup bread crumbs
½ cup wheat germ
½ cup rolled oats
½ tsp thyme
2 Tbsp nutritional yeast
½ cup tomato puree
1 Tbsp vinegar
½ tsp salt

Sauté the onion in the olive oil until soft.

Preheat the oven to 350°.

Add the sautéed onions to the remaining ingredients, and mix well. Press the mixture into a loaf pan, cover with aluminum foil or a cookie sheet, and bake for 20 minutes. Uncover and bake for 10 minutes more.

Per serving: Calories: 216, Protein: 13 gm., Fat: 3 gm., Carbohydrates: 33 gm.

Garbanzo-Vegetable Loaf

Serves 6

This tasty loaf is a treat with mashed potatoes and gravy and a leafy green salad. You'll also enjoy it sliced in a sandwich, if you have any leftovers.

1 cup onions, chopped
3 cloves garlic, minced
1 ½ cups carrots, grated
1 ½ cups celery, finely chopped
1 tsp olive oil

3 ½ cups cooked garbanzo beans, mashed
1 cup whole wheat bread crumbs
¼ cup fresh parsley, minced
½ tsp thyme
½ tsp savory
1 Tbsp tarragon
½ cup apple juice
½ tsp salt

Sauté the onions, garlic, carrots, and celery in the olive oil, stirring constantly, for several minutes.

Preheat the oven to 350°.

Combine all of the ingredients in a bowl, and mix thoroughly. Place the mixture in a lightly oiled bread pan, cover with aluminum foil, and bake for 1 hour. Cool the loaf in the pan before removing.

Per serving: Calories: 226, Protein: 9 gm., Fat: 2 gm., Carbohydrates: 40 gm.

Island Loaf

Serves 6

This loaf is good in sandwiches when it is cold and sliced.

⅓ *cup sunflower seeds,*

3 *cups cooked navy beans, mashed*
1 *cup whole wheat bread crumbs,*
    soft
½ *cup rolled oats*

⅓ *cup pineapple juice, from a can of*
    crushed pineapple (see
    below)
1 *green pepper, chopped*
1 *Tbsp molasses*
1 *Tbsp spicy mustard*
½ *tsp garlic powder*
½ *tsp salt*

1 *(16 oz.) can crushed pineapple,*
    drained

Preheat the oven to 350°.

Use blender to grind seeds into a coarse meal.

Mix together the sunflower seeds, mashed beans, bread crumbs, rolled oats, pineapple juice, pepper, molasses, mustard, garlic powder, and salt. Press the mixture into a lightly oiled loaf pan.

Spread the crushed pineapple over the top of the loaf, and bake for 45 minutes.

Per serving: Calories: 289, Protein: 11 gm., Fat: 5 gm., Carbohydrates: 48 gm.

Stuffed Acorn Squash

Serves 6

3 acorn squash

Cut the squash in half lengthways, and remove the seeds and pulp with a spoon. On each piece, poke the outside skin with a fork to let the steam penetrate. Place the squash in a large pot with ½" water, cover, and steam for 15 minutes.

Sauce:
2 cups tomatoes, canned or fresh
¼ cup tomato paste
¼ cup lemon juice
½ tsp garlic powder

Cook the sauce ingredients together in a saucepan until hot.

Filling:
1½ cups onions, chopped
2 cloves garlic, minced
1 tsp olive oil

In a medium skillet, sauté the onions and garlic in the olive oil until soft.

1 cup tomatoes, chopped,
      or canned tomato puree
1 Tbsp tomato paste
1½ cups cooked rice
1½ cups cooked garbanzo beans
½ tsp cinnamon
¼ tsp clove
1 tsp salt

Add the tomatoes, tomato paste, rice and garbanzo beans, and spices to the skillet, stir well, and cook just enough to heat throughout. Preheat the oven to 350°

To assemble, stuff each squash half with one-sixth of the filling, and place in a 9" x 13" baking dish. Pour the tomato sauce over the squash, cover with aluminum foil, and bake for 30 minutes.

Per serving: Calories: 271, Protein: 7 gm., Fat: 2 gm., Carbohydrates: 55 gm.

Stuffed Cabbage with Black-Eyed Peas

Serves 5-6

This stuffed cabbage is an interesting version of an old favorite

Filling:
1 cup onions, chopped
1 cup celery stalks and leaves, chopped
3 cloves garlic, minced
2 chili peppers, minced (optional)
1 tsp olive oil

In a medium skillet, sauté the onions, celery, garlic, and chili peppers in the olive oil for 5 minutes until soft.

2 cups cooked black-eyed peas
2 cups cooked brown rice
1 tsp cumin
1 tsp coriander

Add the black-eyed peas, rice, and spices to the skillet, and stir well. Cook gently for several minutes to let the flavors blend. Set aside until the cabbage is ready for rolling.

2 cups water (for steaming cabbage)
1 large head cabbage

Put the water in a large, covered pot, and bring to a boil. Meanwhile, remove the core from the head of the cabbage. Peel off the outer leaves one by one without tearing them. Count out 10-12 large leaves, and place them in the boiling water. Steam for 5 minutes to soften the leaves. Save the water. Chop up the smaller leaves and any larger, split leaves to place on the bottom of the baking dish.

Preheat the oven to 350°.

Cook the spaghetti sauce, tomato puree, garlic, basil, and lemon juice for 10 minutes.

To assemble, spread 2 cups of the chopped cabbage on the bottom of a 9" x 13" baking dish. Pour ½ cup of the cabbage liquid over the chopped cabbage.

Put a steamed cabbage leaf on a clean work area. If it is too stiff to roll, cut out a V-shaped section of the core end of the cabbage. Spoon about ⅓ cup of filling onto the center of the cabbage leaf. Fold over two sides of the leaf and, starting with the core end, firmly roll the cabbage over the filling. If the cabbage leaf doesn't overlap, remove some of the filling and re-roll.

Place the cabbage roll seam side down on one edge of the dish lined with the chopped cabbage. Roll up all of the steamed leaves with filling until the baking dish is full. Pour the tomato sauce over all, and bake for 35 minutes.

Sauce:
2 cups spaghetti sauce
3 cups tomato puree
1 tsp garlic powder
1 tsp dried basil
2 Tbsp lemon juice

Per serving: Calories: 297, Protein: 4 gm., Fat: 0 gm., Carbohydrates: 18 gm.

Soy Stuffed Peppers

Serves 6

4 large peppers

Cut the peppers lengthwise, remove the stems and seeds, place in a deep pan, and cover with boiling water. Cover the pan and let stand while preparing the filling.

1 cup onions, chopped
½ cup celery, chopped
1 cup carrots, shredded
1 tsp canola oil

Sauté the onions, celery, and carrots in the canola oil for several minutes until soft.

Filling:
2 cups cooked soybeans
2 cups cooked brown rice or millet
1 cup tomatoes, chopped
½ tsp garlic powder
¼ tsp thyme
¼ tsp basil
½ tsp salt
¼ tsp black pepper
¼ cup fresh parsley, chopped

Add the soybeans, rice or millet, tomatoes, and spices to the pan with the onions, celery, and carrots, and cook on low heat for 5 minutes.

Preheat the oven to 350°.

2 cups spaghetti sauce

Remove the peppers from the water, and stuff each half with several heaping tablespoons of the filling.

Place the stuffed peppers in a shallow 9" x 13" baking dish, and pour the spaghetti sauce around (not over) the peppers.

Topping:
2 Tbsp nutritional yeast
2 Tbsp wheat germ

Sprinkle with the topping, and bake for 40 minutes.

Per serving: Calories: 261, Protein: 12 gm., Fat: 6 gm., Carbohydrates: 40 gm.

Tamale Stuffed Peppers

Serves 6

6 green or red bell peppers

Slice the tops off the peppers, and remove the seeds. Blanch them in 1" of boiling water for 5 minutes, drain, and set aside while you prepare the filling.

1 cup onions, chopped
3 cloves garlic, minced
1 tsp canola oil

In a medium skillet, sauté the onions and garlic in the canola oil until soft.

3 cups tomatoes, chopped
¾ cup cornmeal
1½ Tbsp chili powder
1½ tsp cumin
½ tsp salt

Add the tomatoes, cornmeal, chili powder, cumin, and salt to the sautéed onions and garlic, and cook until thick, stirring constantly.

Preheat the oven to 350°.

2 cups cooked black beans
1½ cups frozen corn

Add the black beans and corn to the skillet, and cook until hot. Fill each steamed pepper with one-sixth of the filling. Put them upright in a shallow baking dish, pour ½" of water into the baking dish, and bake for 25 minutes.

Per serving: Calories: 225, Protein: 8 gm., Fat: 2 gm., Carbohydrates: 44 gm.

Black Eyed Spirals

Yields 12-14

This is an easy quick-dough recipe filled with tasty beans and vegetables. These rolls are good warm for supper but also make good picnic or lunch food.

Dough:
1½ cups lukewarm water
1 package yeast (1 Tbsp)
2 Tbsp honey
1 cup unbleached white flour

1 Tbsp canola oil
¼ tsp salt
1½ cups unbleached white flour
1½ cups whole wheat flour
¼ cup wheat germ

Filling:
1 cup dried tomatoes
½ cup boiling water

*3 cups spinach, collards, or kale,
     chopped, cooked, and drained*
2 Tbsp garlic, minced (5-6 cloves)
¼ cup lemon juice
½ cup fresh parsley, chopped
2 tsp crushed dill
2 Tbsp soy sauce
*3 cups cooked black-eyed peas,
     drained and mashed*

In a medium mixing bowl, whisk together the warm water, yeast, honey, and flour, and let sit 10 minutes until bubbly.

Add the canola oil, salt, flours, and wheat germ to the bubbly yeast mixture, and mix with a wooden spoon. On a lightly floured surface, knead for 5 minutes until a smooth dough is formed. Add more flour if the dough is too sticky, but keep the dough soft and satiny. Put in a lightly oiled bowl, cover with a damp cloth, and prepare the filling.

Soak the dried tomatoes in boiling water for 10-15 minutes, and drain.

With a fork, thoroughly mix the tomatoes, greens, garlic, lemon juice, parsley, dill, soy sauce, and black-eyed peas, or combine in a food processor for a smoother consistency.
When the filling is well blended, roll out the dough on a lightly floured surface into a 15" square, about ¼" thick. Spoon the filling out to cover the surface, leaving a ½" margin around

the edges. Starting with the edge, roll the dough around the filling as if you were making cinnamon rolls. Make a roll. With a sharp knife, cut the log into 1" spirals, and place them on a lightly oiled cookie sheet. As you transfer the spirals to the baking sheet, you may need to pinch the dough back together to make them round again. While your rolls are rising (10-15 minutes), preheat the oven to 350°. Bake for 20-25 minutes.

Per serving: Calories: 218, Protein: 8 gm., Fat: 2 gm., Carbohydrates: 42 gm.

Eggplant Rolls

Makes 16 rolls

2 medium eggplants

Cut each eggplant lengthways into ¼" thick slices, and steam for 8-10 minutes until flexible. Drain in a colander.

Filling:
3 cups cooked pinto beans, mashed
1 tsp garlic powder
1 Tbsp chili powder
1 tsp cumin, ground
½ tsp salt
⅓ cup wheat germ

Combine the beans with the garlic powder, chili powder, cumin, salt, and wheat germ, and mix well to form a thick paste.

Sauce:
3 cups tomato juice or puree
1 Tbsp lemon juice
1 tsp paprika
1 Tbsp soy sauce
½ tsp dried chili pepper (optional)

In a saucepan, heat the tomato juice, lemon juice, paprika, soy sauce, and chili pepper.

Preheat the oven to 350°.

To assemble, put a drained eggplant slice on a clean work area. Spoon 2 tablespoons of pinto filling onto the narrow edge of the eggplant. Roll the eggplant around the filling, and place in a 10" square baking pan with the rolled edge facing up. When all the rolls are in place, pour the tomato sauce over the top, and bake for 45 minutes.

Per serving: Calories: 92, Protein: 4 gm., Fat: 0 gm., Carbohydrates: 18 gm.

Bean Sausage Links

Yields 36 links

These little links are good for breakfast, lunch, or dinner. Mix up the whole batch, and cook them as needed. You might want to freeze part of the mix to have another time. We like to eat these with bagels.

**2 cups cooked soybeans, mashed
(3 cups cooked)
1 cup cooked lima beans, mashed
1 cup cooked navy beans, mashed**

Mash the beans together or puree in a food processor.

Preheat the oven to 450°.

**½ cup wheat germ
½ cup whole wheat flour
½ cup nutritional yeast
1½ tsp fennel seeds
½ tsp black pepper
4 tsp garlic powder
½ tsp salt
1 tsp allspice
3 tsp oregano
½ tsp cayenne pepper
1½ Tbsp brown sugar
2 Tbsp soy sauce
2 Tbsp wet mustard**

Combine the rest of the ingredients with the pureed beans, mix well, and shape into finger-sized links or small patties. Bake on an oiled cookie sheet until browned, about 20-30 minutes. Turn over once during baking.

Per 2 links: Calories: 109, Protein: 7 gm., Fat: 2 gm., Carbohydrates: 16 gm.

Falafel

Yields twenty 1" balls

These balls can be served in pita bread with fresh vegetables, soy yogurt, and tahini sauce as toppings. These falafels are baked instead of fried and therefore lower in fat. If you have any leftovers, they can be flattened and used in sandwiches

3 cups cooked garbanzo beans
1 small onion, finely chopped
¼ tsp garlic powder
¼ cup parsley, minced
1 tsp paprika
1 Tbsp soy sauce
2 Tbsp wheat germ
¼ cup whole wheat flour

Combine all of the ingredients in a food processor, or mash in a bowl and mix well.

Preheat the oven to 350°.

Wet hands and form into 1" balls.

Bake on a lightly oiled cookie sheet for 10 minutes on one side and 10 minutes on the other.

Per two balls: Calories: 101, Protein: 5 gm., Fat: 1 gm., Carbohydrates: 17 gm.

Pinto Burgers

Yields 12 burgers

These burgers are great for a quick supper when the kids are in and out. I like to keep leftover cooked oatmeal around to use as an egg substitute in cakes and cookies and for recipes like this.

⅔ cup dry textured vegetable protein granules
½ cup boiling water

Place the textured vegetable protein in a small bowl, cover with the boiling water, and let sit for 10 minutes.

1 tsp garlic powder
½ tsp oregano
½ tsp chili powder
⅛ tsp black pepper
2 tsp soy sauce

Add the spices and soy sauce, and mix well.

⅔ cup onions, minced
½ tsp oil

Sauté the onions in the oil for a few minutes, stirring frequently to prevent sticking.

2 cups cooked pinto beans, mashed
¾ cup cooked (cold) oatmeal

While the textured vegetable protein is soaking and the onions are cooking, mix the pinto beans and oatmeal in a medium bowl. Combine all of the ingredients thoroughly. Wet hands with cold water, and pat mixture into thin burgers. Fry on a skillet with as much or as little oil as you want.

Per burger: Calories: 73, Protein: 5 gm., Fat: 0 gm., Carbohydrates: 12 gm.

Lentil Burgers

Yields 8 burgers

1 cup lentils
3 cups water

In a medium saucepan, bring the lentils and water to a boil, lower the heat, cover, and cook for 30 minutes until tender. Drain.

1 small onion, finely chopped
4 mushrooms (⅓ cup), chopped
1 stalk celery, minced
1 Tbsp water

In a medium skillet, steam the onion, mushrooms, and celery in the water, stirring to prevent sticking.

½ tsp garlic powder
1 tsp oregano
½ tsp thyme
½ tsp sage
¼ tsp salt
¼ cup unbleached flour
¼ cup rolled oats or bread crumbs
2 Tbsp peanut butter or tahini
1 tsp prepared mustard

Mix all of the ingredients together. Shape into patties and cook on a skillet, or bake in a 350° oven for 20 minutes. Turn once to brown on both sides.

Per burger: Calories: 111, Protein: 6 gm., Fat: 2 gm., Carbohydrates: 17 gm.

Soy Burgers

Yields 12 burgers

These are a favorite with us. They can be made into patties ahead of time and refrigerated until you're ready to cook. Serve them on buns with lettuce or sprouts and tomato.

4 cups cooked soybeans
½ cup onions, chopped,
      or 1 tsp onion powder
1 Tbsp soy sauce
1 tsp garlic powder
½ tsp oregano
⅓ cup wheat germ
¼ cup fresh parsley, chopped,
      or 1 Tbsp dried parsley

Mash the soybeans with a potato masher or in a food processor. Mix all of the other ingredients with the mashed soybeans. Wet your hands to keep the dough from sticking to them, and form into patties. Cook on a hot, lightly oiled skillet until brown on both sides.

Per burger: Calories: 94, Protein: 8 gm., Fat: 4 gm., Carbohydrates: 8 gm.

Pinto Pies

Makes 4 individual pies

1 cup cooked pinto beans, mashed
1 tomato, finely chopped
1 small onion, minced
¼ cup green pepper, minced
1 Tbsp lemon juice
2 Tbsp fresh parsley, minced
½ tsp garlic powder
¼ tsp basil
¼ tsp oregano
½ tsp salt
pinch of crushed red pepper

2 pita breads

Mix the mashed beans with all the other ingredients until well blended.

Preheat the oven to 350°.

Separate each pita bread into two rounds. Place them side by side on a cookie sheet. Spread one-fourth of the bean mixture evenly to the edges of each pita round. Bake for 8-10 minutes until the pitas are crisp.

Per serving: Calories: 150, Protein: 6 gm., Fat: 1 gm., Carbohydrates: 29 gm.

Meatless Pinto Balls

Yields 24 balls

Try these with spaghetti. They make good sandwich fillers if you have any leftover.

2½ cups cooked pinto beans
¾ cup bread crumbs
¼ cup nutritional yeast
¼ cup fresh parsley, chopped
2 Tbsp soy sauce
½ cup onions, minced
1 tsp garlic powder
½ tsp celery seed
1 tsp basil
¼ tsp allspice

Put all of the ingredients in a medium mixing bowl. Mix with your hands until thoroughly combined. Break off little pieces, roll into 1" balls, and cook on a lightly oiled skillet. Cover while cooking and turn a few times to brown on several sides.

Per ball: Calories: 35, Protein: 2 gm., Fat: 0 gm., Carbohydrates: 6 gm.

Curried Veggie Fritters

Yields fourteen 3" fritters

These crunchy, curried fritters are good for travel food, bag lunches, or supper. I like them cooked with just a drop of oil, but you can make them crispier by using more oil. Have some chutney on hand to serve with them.

½ cup carrot, grated
½ cup onions, minced
1 cup celery, chopped
1 Tbsp soy sauce
1 cup cooked pinto beans, mashed
½ cup water

In a medium mixing bowl, combine the carrot, onions, celery, soy sauce, mashed beans, and water.

¼ tsp coriander
¼ tsp cardamom
1 tsp cumin
½ tsp garlic powder
½ cup chick-pea flour
1 tsp baking powder

Sift the coriander, cardamom, cumin, garlic powder, chick-pea flour, and baking powder into the bowl of mashed pinto beans and veggies, and stir to combine well. With damp hands, pat into flat, 3" round patties. Cook on a lightly oiled, medium-hot skillet. Turn when the first side is lightly browned. They may also be baked on cookie sheets in a 350° oven for 10 minutes on each side.

Per fritter: Calories: 42, Protein: 2 gm., Fat: 0 gm., Carbohydrates: 8 gm.

Autumn Stew

Serves 4-6

¾ cup onions, chopped
1 large clove garlic, chopped
1 tsp oil

5 cups water
¼ cup yellow split peas
½ cup dried lima beans
½ cup dry bulgur
2 cups sweet potatoes cubed
2 cups cabbage, chopped
1 Tbsp soy sauce
¼ tsp rosemary

In a soup pot, sauté the onions and garlic in the oil until soft.

Add the remaining ingredients to the pot, bring to a boil, lower the heat, cover, and simmer for an hour, stirring occasionally. Test to see if the beans are soft. Continue to cook if necessary.

Per serving: Calories: 214, Protein: 7 gm., Fat: 1 gm., Carbohydrates: 43 gm.

Lentil-Vegetable Biryani

Serves 4-6

This potpourri of vegetables, spices, and lentils, produces a dish you'll not forget. Serve this when you have company and you want something especially nutritious and delicious.

1 cup onions, chopped
½ tsp canola oil

In a heavy soup pot, sauté the onions in the canola oil until golden brown.

2 chili peppers, minced
1½" piece gingerroot, grated
8 cloves garlic, minced

Add the chili peppers, gingerroot, and garlic to the pot, and stir for several minutes.

¾ cup lentils, soaked
1½ cups water
1 cup green beans, chopped
1 cup carrots, sliced
2 large tomatoes, chopped,
*   or 2 cups canned tomatoes*
4 whole cloves
1 stick cinnamon
½ tsp cardamom
1 tsp turmeric

Add the lentils, water, green beans, carrots, tomatoes, and spices to the pot. Bring to a boil, lower heat, cover, and cook for 15 minutes.

1 cup basmati, white rice
3 potatoes, large cut into ½" cubes
3 cups hot water
1 cup fresh or frozen peas
2 Tbsp fresh mint, minced,
*   or ½ tsp dried mint*
½ tsp salt

Add the rice, potatoes, water, peas, mint, and salt; cover and cook 25-30 minutes until the rice is done. Let sit for several minutes before serving.

Per serving: Calories: 332, Protein: 11 gm., Fat: 1 gm., Carbohydrates: 69 gm.

Spanish Stew

Serves 6

4 cloves garlic, minced
1 onion, thinly sliced
2 cups mushrooms, sliced
1 cup cabbage, thinly sliced
1 tsp olive oil

In a soup pot, sauté the garlic, onion, mushrooms, and cabbage in the olive oil until the cabbage and mushrooms are soft.

3 cups stewed tomatoes
1 bay leaf
2 carrots, thinly sliced
1 potato, diced into bite-sized pieces

Add the tomatoes, bay leaf, carrots, and potato to the sautéed vegetables. Bring to a boil, lower to a simmer, cover, and cook for 15 minutes.

2 cups garbanzo beans
2 Tbsp fresh parsley, minced
1 Tbsp fresh mint, chopped
1 tsp dried oregano
1 tsp salt
⅛ tsp black pepper

Add the beans, parsley, mint, oregano, salt, and black pepper to the stew, and simmer for 10 minutes.

Per serving: Calories: 193, Protein: 6 gm., Fat: 2 gm., Carbohydrates: 36 gm.

White Bean and Squash Stew

Serves 4-6
This is good served over rice or bulgur.

3 cups water
1½ cups white beans

In a large soup pot, cook the beans for 30 minutes.

2 medium potatoes, chopped
2 cups winter squash or pumpkin, cubed
2 leeks, chopped
1 large onion, chopped
2 cloves garlic, chopped
1 cup chopped tomato, fresh or canned

Add the potatoes, squash or pumpkin, leeks, onion, garlic, and tomato to the beans. Continue cooking for 30-45 minutes until the beans and vegetables are soft.

3 Tbsp tomato paste
juice of 2 lemons
¼ cup fresh parsley, chopped
½ tsp dill seed
1 tsp salt

Add the tomato paste, lemon juice, parsley, dill seed, and salt, and simmer for 10 more minutes. Keep covered until ready to serve.

Per serving: Calories: 288, Protein: 12 gm., Fat: 0 gm., Carbohydrates: 58 gm.

Kidney-Polenta Stew

Serves 6

Leftover polenta is delicious the next day. It congeals when cold, so you can slice and lightly fry it, topping with a little tomato sauce, if desired.

1 bay leaf
¾ cup onions, chopped
¾ cup celery, chopped
2 cloves garlic, chopped
1 Tbsp soy sauce
¾ cup cornmeal
1 quart of water

In a thick-bottomed soup pot, cook the bay leaf, onion, celery, garlic, soy sauce, and cornmeal in the water for 20 minutes, stirring occasionally.

2 cups cooked kidney beans
1 (10 oz.) package frozen spinach, thawed
½ tsp salt

Add the kidney beans, spinach, and salt, and continue heating until hot. Serve immediately.

Per serving: Calories: 160, Protein: 7 gm., Fat: 0 gm., Carbohydrates: 31 gm.

Lentil Stew

Serves 6

1 cup onions, chopped
½ cup celery, chopped
½ cup carrots, diced
1 tsp olive oil

In a soup pot, sauté the onions, celery, and carrots in the olive oil until soft.

4 cups water
1 cup lentils
½ tsp oregano
½ tsp thyme
1 tsp basil

Add the water, lentils, and herbs to the sautéed vegetables. Bring to a boil, cover, and simmer for 45 minutes.

1 medium eggplant, cubed
1 tsp oil

While the lentils are cooking, cook the eggplant in the oil in a medium skillet, turning frequently to lightly brown on all sides.

1 (6 oz.) can tomato paste
¼ cup red wine vinegar
¼ tsp cinnamon
½ tsp salt
pinch of crushed red pepper

After the lentils are soft, add the browned eggplant, tomato paste, vinegar, cinnamon, salt, and red pepper, and cook on low heat for 10 minutes. Add a little water if needed.

Per serving: Calories: 149, Protein: 7 gm., Fat: 1 gm., Carbohydrates: 28 gm.

Kidney-Yam Stew

Serves 6

5 cups water
½ cup brown rice
1 medium onion, chopped
2 cloves garlic, minced
1 green pepper, chopped
1 cup fresh or canned tomato, chopped
2 cups yam or sweet potato, cubed
2 medium white potatoes, cubed
1 cup green beans, chopped
      (if using canned green beans,
      add later with corn and
      kidney beans)
1 cup cabbage, diced
1 jalapeño pepper, minced (optional)

In a large soup pot, combine the water, rice, onion, garlic, green pepper, tomato, potatoes, green beans, cabbage, and jalapeño pepper. Cover, bring to a boil, and simmer for 30 minutes.

2 cups cooked kidney beans
1 cup fresh or frozen corn
¼ cup fresh parsley or coriander
      or a combination of both
1 tsp salt

Add the kidney beans, corn, parsley and/or coriander, and salt, and continue to simmer for 15 more minutes, stirring occasionally. Add some bean stock or water if the stew is too thick.

Per serving: Calories: 275, Protein: 8 gm., Fat: 0 gm., Carbohydrates: 59 gm.

Garbanzo-Sweet Potato Stew

Serves 6

This stew is good served over couscous or brown rice.

1 cup onions, chopped
1 cup red or green pepper, chopped
1½ chili peppers, minced
1 tsp olive oil

In a heavy pan, sauté the onions and peppers in the olive oil until soft.

2 cups tomatoes, chopped
¼ cup water
2 cups sweet potato, peeled and cubed
½ tsp cinnamon
½ tsp coriander
½ tsp cardamom

Add the tomatoes, water, sweet potatoes, and spices to the pan, cover, and simmer for 10 minutes.

2 cups cooked garbanzo beans
**   [1 (15 oz.) can]**
2 cups zucchini, chopped
juice of one lemon
½ tsp salt

Add the garbanzo beans, zucchini, lemon juice, and salt, cover, and continue to cook for 10 more minutes.

Per serving: Calories: 182, Protein: 6 gm., Fat: 2 gm., Carbohydrates: 35 gm.

Easy White Bean Stew

Serves 6

This recipe is designed to use up some leftover beans.

2 cups stock or water
1 cup carrots, chopped
2 potatoes, cubed
1 bay leaf

In a soup pot, bring the stock to a boil, add the carrots, potatoes, and bay leaf, and simmer for 5-10 minutes.

3 cloves garlic, minced
1 cup onions, chopped
1 cup mushrooms, chopped in half
1 cup peppers, chopped
2 cups cabbage, sliced
1 tsp canola oil

While the stock is simmering, sauté the garlic, onions, mushrooms, peppers, and cabbage in the canola oil in a medium skillet. Add to the soup pot when the cabbage is soft (about 5 minutes).

2 cups cooked white beans
1 Tbsp lemon juice
1 tsp thyme
1 Tbsp chervil
½ tsp salt
pepper to taste

Stir in the beans, lemon juice, thyme, chervil, salt, and pepper, and simmer for 5 minutes. Turn off the heat, cover, and let sit for 15 minutes before serving.

Per serving: Calories: 165, Protein: 6 gm., Fat: 0 gm., Carbohydrates: 32 gm.

Lentils 'n Barley

Serves 4

The texture in this dish makes it stand out.

1½ cups tomato juice
1 cup water
½ cup lentils
⅓ cup barley

Simmer the tomato juice, water, lentils, and barley together for 15 minutes.

1 cup celery, chopped
½ cup onions, chopped
½ cup carrots, chopped
½ cup potatoes, cubed small
½ tsp savory
½ tsp chervil
½ tsp thyme
½ tsp tarragon

Add the celery, onions, carrots, potatoes, and herbs to the lentils and barley, and simmer for 25 minutes, stirring occasionally. If it sticks to the bottom of the pan add a little more water.

Per serving: Calories: 128, Protein: 5 gm., Fat: 0 gm., Carbohydrates: 27 gm.

Sweet 'n Sour Garbanzo Medley

Serves 6

Pineapple sauce:
**1 (20 oz.) can pineapple chunks
in unsweetened juice
3 Tbsp cornstarch
⅓ cup cider vinegar
¼ cup honey
½ tsp garlic powder**

Drain the pineapple juice into a small saucepan or bowl, and combine with the cornstarch, vinegar, honey, and garlic powder. Add the pineapple chunks and set aside.

**½ Tbsp gingerroot, grated
¾ cup onions, chopped
1 bell pepper, cut into thin strips
1 cup carrots, diced
2 cups zucchini, sliced
1 tsp canola oil**

In a large skillet, stir-fry the gingerroot, onions, bell pepper, carrots, and zucchini in the canola oil for 5 minutes.

**2 cups mung bean sprouts
2 cups cooked garbanzo beans
¼ cup water
2 Tbsp soy sauce**

Add the sprouts, garbanzo beans, water, and soy sauce to the skillet, cover, and simmer for 10 minutes. Uncover and add the pineapple sauce, stirring while the mixture thickens. When it comes to a boil, cover and turn off the heat. Serve over rice or millet.

Per serving: Calories: 256, Protein: 7 gm., Fat: 2 gm., Carbohydrates: 52 gm.

Barbecue Soybeans

Serves 8

Here's a delicious way to serve soy beans . . . or use any bean of your choice.

1 cup onions, chopped
3 cloves garlic, minced,
**   or 1 tsp garlic powder**
1 tsp canola oil

In a large skillet, sauté the onions and garlic in the canola oil until they begin to brown.

3 cups water
1 (6 oz.) can tomato paste
⅓ cup brown sugar or honey
1 Tbsp molasses
2 Tbsp soy sauce
½ tsp allspice
½ tsp salt
1-2 crushed red peppers
**   or 1-1½ tsp dried red pepper**
¼ cup vinegar

Add the water, tomato paste, sweeteners, soy sauce, spices, and vinegar to the skillet, and cook for 15 minutes.

4 cups cooked soybeans

Add the beans to the sauce, and cook for 15-20 minutes to let the beans absorb the flavor of the sauce. Serve over rice.

Per serving: Calories: 201, Protein: 11 gm., Fat: 5 gm., Carbohydrates: 27 gm.

Lentils and Eggplant

Serves 5

Serve this sweet and sour lentil sauce over rice, millet, or couscous.

1 cup lentils
3 cups water

In a medium saucepan, bring the lentils and water to a boil; then lower the heat, cover, and simmer for 30 minutes.

1 medium eggplant, cubed
½ cup whole wheat flour

Put the eggplant in a medium bowl, sprinkle with flour, and mix well until the eggplant is coated.

1 Tbsp oil
1 cup onions, cut in thin crescents

Heat the oil in a large skillet, add the onions and coated eggplant, and stir while cooking until the eggplant is browned.

1½ cups tomato juice,
     or tomato puree
2 Tbsp soy sauce
2 Tbsp cider vinegar
1 Tbsp honey
½ tsp garlic powder
1 tsp chili powder

Add the tomato juice, soy sauce, vinegar, honey, and spices to the onion/eggplant mixture, and simmer for 15 minutes. Add the lentils, cover, and continue to cook on low heat for 20 more minutes until the lentils are quite soft.

Per serving: Calories: 218, Protein: 9 gm., Fat: 3 gm., Carbohydrates: 38 gm.

Tanzanian Kidneys with Coconut

Serves 6

Fresh coconut is best but use dried if fresh isn't available.

2 cups potatoes, peeled and cubed

Boil the potatoes until soft but not mushy.

3 cloves garlic, minced
½ tsp canola oil

In a large skillet, sauté the garlic in the canola oil.

2 tsp coriander
2 tsp cumin
2 tsp turmeric
½ tsp salt
1 chili pepper, minced,
**   or ¾ tsp dried chili pepper**
juice of 1 lime
½ cup bean stock
½ cup coconut, grated
5 cups cooked kidney beans

Add the coriander, cumin, turmeric, salt, chili pepper, lime juice, bean stock, and coconut to sautéed garlic, and cook over medium heat until bubbly. Add the cooked kidney beans and potatoes, cover, and cook over low heat for several minutes. Serve hot over rice.

Per serving: Calories: 361, Protein: 13 gm., Fat: 13 gm., Carbohydrates: 49 gm.

Spicy Lentils

Serves 6

2 cups lentils
8 cups water

1 large onion, chopped
1 tsp garlic, minced
1 tsp olive oil

1 tsp fresh gingerroot, grated
1 tsp ground coriander
1 tsp cumin
1 tsp cardamom
½ tsp chili pepper
½ tsp salt
1 large tomato, chopped

In a medium saucepan, bring the lentils and water to a boil, lower the heat, cover, and simmer for 40 minutes. Drain.

While the lentils are cooking, sauté the onion and garlic in the olive oil in a large cooking pot.

Add the remaining spices and tomato to the garlic and onions, and simmer for 3 minutes. Add the cooked lentils and heat slowly until the mixture is thick. Serve over rice.

Per serving: Calories: 173, Protein: 11 gm., Fat: 1 gm., Carbohydrates: 30 gm.

Sweet and Sour Soybeans

Serves 4

How can soybeans taste exotic? Try this recipe and see.

1 clove garlic, minced
1 onion, chopped
1 cup celery, chopped
1 cup green pepper, chopped
1 tsp oil

In a 10" skillet, sauté the garlic, onion, celery, and green pepper in the oil until soft.

2 cups cooked soybeans
1 (20 oz.) can unsweetened
    pineapple chunks (save juice)

Add the soybeans and pineapple to the skillet after the vegetables are cooked.

1½ Tbsp cornstarch
¼ tsp ground ginger
2 Tbsp soy sauce
¼ cup vinegar
¾ cup pineapple juice

Combine the cornstarch, ginger, soy sauce, vinegar, and pineapple juice in a jar with a tight fitting lid, and shake vigorously until well mixed. Pour over the vegetable/bean mixture, and heat until thick, stirring constantly. Gently boil a few minutes. Serve over rice.

Per serving: Calories: 255, Protein: 12 gm., Fat: 7 gm., Carbohydrates: 39 gm.

Garbanzo Gumbo

Serves 6

You can use fresh or frozen okra for this colorful dish. Our southern cousins will be proud of this alternative to their familiar stew.

1 cup onions, chopped
3 cloves garlic, minced
4 cups okra, sliced in ½" rounds
1 green pepper, chopped
1 green chili pepper, finely chopped
1 tsp olive oil

Sauté the onions, garlic, okra, green pepper, and chili pepper in the olive oil for 5 minutes.

3 cups fresh or canned tomatoes, chopped
½ cup fresh parsley, chopped
¼ cup fresh basil leaves, chopped, or ½ tsp dried basil

Add the tomatoes, parsley, and basil, cover, and simmer until the okra is tender.

3 cups cooked garbanzo beans
1½ cups bean stock
½ tsp salt
3 Tbsp lemon juice

Add the garbanzo beans and enough stock to make a gravy, bring to a boil, and add the salt and lemon juice. Simmer for a few minutes, and keep hot until ready to serve. Serve over rice.

Per serving: Calories: 202, Protein: 9 gm., Fat: 2 gm., Carbohydrates: 35 gm.

Curried Garbanzos

Serves 4-6

This is a sweet and spicy dish that you'll want to make again and again. It's also good as a cold leftover; you can mash it and use it as a sandwich spread.

1 large onion, chopped
3 cloves garlic, minced
1 tsp gingerroot, minced
1 tsp canola oil

Sauté the onion, garlic, and gingerroot in the canola oil until the onion is transparent.

2 medium potatoes, cubed small
1 cup fresh or canned tomatoes, chopped

Add the potatoes and tomatoes, cover, and cook for 5 minutes.

2 cups cooked garbanzo beans
1 cup garbanzo stock
4 Tbsp tomato paste
1 cup stewed tomatoes
½ tsp salt
¼ tsp black pepper

Combine the garbanzo beans, stock, tomato paste, stewed tomatoes, salt, and black pepper with the onion/potato mixture; bring to a boil and lower heat to a simmer. Cook for 10 minutes, stirring occasionally. Serve over rice or millet.

Per serving: Calories: 214, Protein: 7 gm., Fat: 2 gm., Carbohydrates: 40 gm.

Bean Sprout Curry

Serves 4-6

A delicious curry that is good with your favorite dal or a tossed salad and rice.

¾ cup onions, chopped
1 clove garlic, minced
1 tsp gingerroot, grated
1 tsp oil

Sauté the onions, garlic, and gingerroot in the oil for a few minutes.

3 medium potatoes, chopped into
½" cubes
½ cup water
¾ cup fresh or canned tomatoes,
chopped

Add the potatoes, water, and tomatoes to the skillet; cover and cook 10-15 minutes until the potatoes are almost soft.

½ tsp salt
¼ tsp black pepper
1 ½ tsp Garam Masala (see page 108)
2 ½ cups mung bean or lentil sprouts
(see page 108)

Add the spices and sprouts to the skillet, cover, and simmer 2-3 minutes until the sprouts are wilted but not soft. Serve over rice.

Per serving: Calories: 139, Protein: 3 gm., Fat: 1 gm., Carbohydrates: 28 gm.

Sprouted Lentils

Yield 4 cups

½ cup lentils
2 cups water

In a wide-mouth, quart glass jar, soak the lentils overnight or for 8 hours. Attach a piece of cheesecloth or wire screen over the mouth of the jar, and drain well. Rinse every morning and night for 4-5 days. If the room temperature is 70° or higher, the sprouts will grow faster and may need to be rinsed more frequently.

The sprouts are done when the first leaves begin to appear. If you aren't ready to use the sprouts right away, drain them well and refrigerate them right away so they won't spoil.

Per ½ cup: Calories: 40, Protein: 2 gm., Fat: 0 gm., Carbohydrates: 8 gm.

Garam Masala

A sweet/spicy blend of ground spices used to flavor vegetable and bean dishes.

4 tsp coriander
1 tsp black pepper
2 tsp cumin
1 tsp cloves
1 tsp cinnamon
1 tsp cardamom

Combine the spices in a small jar with a tight fitting lid, and shake well to mix thoroughly. Label the jar and store with your spices until ready to use.

Soybean Stroganoff

Serves 4

This is so easy to prepare. Serve with a fresh green salad and your choice of pasta for a tasty dinner.

1 cup onions, diced
8 oz. fresh mushrooms, chopped
        (2½ cups)
½ tsp olive oil

In a medium skillet, sauté the onions and mushrooms in the olive oil until soft.

1 Tbsp cornstarch
⅛ tsp black pepper
3 Tbsp soy sauce

In a bowl or cup, dissolve the cornstarch and black pepper in the soy sauce. Add the paste to the mushrooms and onions, and stir well until it begins to bubble, and a smooth gravy is formed.

2 cups cooked soybeans
1 cup soymilk or soy yogurt

Add the soybeans and soymilk or soy yogurt, and heat only to a simmer. Don't boil the sauce or it may separate into curds and whey. Serve over pasta.

Per serving: Calories: 186, Protein: 14 gm., Fat: 7 gm., Carbohydrates: 19 gm.

Armenian Beans

Serves 4-6

This bean dish is intended to be an accompaniment to a large meal. Have you ever tried to recreate a down-home farm dinner with so many dishes they barely all fit on the table: biscuits and gravy, applesauce, pickles, green salad, succotash, cole slaw, beans, and stewed tomatoes?

1 cup dried baby lima beans
3 cups water

Soak the beans overnight or use the quick soak method (see page 9). Drain the soak water, and bring the lima beans and water to a boil. Lower the heat, cover, and simmer until tender (about 30-35 minutes).

1 carrot, thinly sliced
1 stalk celery, chopped
1 clove garlic, minced
½ tsp olive oil

In a small skillet, sauté the carrot, celery, and garlic in the olive oil for a few minutes, and add to the cooked beans.

2 Tbsp fresh parsley, chopped
1 Tbsp fresh dill weed, minced
½ tsp salt
¼ tsp black pepper

Add the parsley, dill, salt, and black pepper, and simmer for 5 minutes. Cover and keep warm until ready to serve.

Per serving: Calories: 102, Protein: 5 gm., Fat: 0 gm., Carbohydrates: 19 gm.

Curried Limas

Serves 6
This dish is good served over rice or bulgur.

1 onion, chopped
2 cloves garlic, chopped
1 tsp oil

In a medium skillet, sauté the onion and garlic in the oil until they are browned.

4 cups cooked lima beans
½ cup bean stock
2 cups apples, chopped
2 Tbsp soy sauce
1 tsp paprika
1 tsp coriander
1 tsp cumin
½ tsp turmeric
½ tsp ground ginger
1 Tbsp lemon juice

Add the lima beans, bean stock, apples, soy sauce, spices, and lemon juice to the skillet. Cook for 15 minutes until the apples are soft, stirring occasionally.

Per serving: Calories: 214, Protein: 9 gm., Fat: 0 gm., Carbohydrates: 41 gm.

Summer Lentils and Veggies

Serves 6

1 cup dried lentils (½ lb.)
4 cups water

In a medium saucepan, bring the lentils and water to a boil; lower the heat, cover, and cook the lentils until they are soft (about 40 minutes). Drain.

1 onion, chopped
2 cups cauliflower, broken into bite-sized pieces
2 cups fresh green beans, cut into 1" lengths
1 medium zucchini, chopped
1½ cups tomatoes, chopped
1 tsp olive oil

In a large skillet, sauté the onion, cauliflower, green beans, zucchini, and tomatoes in the olive oil, and cook until tender but not mushy.

2 Tbsp parsley, chopped
1 Tbsp basil, chopped
1 Tbsp dill weed, crushed
1 Tbsp soy sauce

Add the herbs and soy sauce to the skillet while the vegetables are cooking. Add the cooked lentils and stir well. This is good served with corn bread.

Per serving: Calories: 129, Protein: 7 gm., Fat: 1 gm., Carbohydrates: 23 gm.

Ceci all' Italiana

(Garbanzos Italian)
Serves 6

2 cups (½ lb.) uncooked shells,
    spirals, or elbows

Cook the pasta, drain, and set aside in a covered pot to keep hot while preparing the garbanzo sauce.

1 onion, chopped
2 cloves garlic, minced
1 head of cauliflower, broken into
    flowerets,
      or 1 (10 oz.) package frozen
      cauliflower
⅛ tsp crushed chili peppers
1 tsp olive oil

In a large skillet, sauté the onion, garlic, cauliflower, and chili peppers in the olive oil for 3-5 minutes.

4 cups fresh or canned tomatoes,
    chopped
1 Tbsp wine vinegar
2 cups cooked garbanzo beans
1 tsp oregano
1 tsp basil
¼ cup fresh parsley, chopped
1 tsp salt
¾ cup black olives, chopped (optional)

Add the tomatoes, vinegar, garbanzo beans, oregano, basil, parsley, salt, and olives to the skillet; cover and simmer until the cauliflower is soft. Pour the sauce over the pasta, mix well, and serve immediately.

Per serving: Calories: 247, Protein: 10 gm., Fat: 2 gm., Carbohydrates: 46 gm.

Black-Eyed Peas with Greens

Serves 6

1 onion, chopped
1 small chili pepper, minced,
        or ¼ tsp dried chili pepper
1 tsp olive oil

1 cup bean stock
4 cups greens, chopped (spinach, beet
        greens, or kale)
¼ tsp allspice
½ cup raisins
1 Tbsp soy sauce
5 cups cooked black-eyed peas

In a medium skillet, sauté the onion and chili pepper in the olive oil.

Add the bean stock, greens, allspice, raisins, soy sauce, and black-eyed peas; cover and cook for 5-10 minutes until the greens are soft. Serve over rice.

Per serving: Calories: 242, Protein: 11 gm., Fat: 2 gm., Carbohydrates: 45 gm.

Brazilian Black Beans

Serves 6-8

This combination of black beans, Spanish rice, kale, and marinated onions is derived from Brazilian traditional cuisine. It's a complete meal served on a platter from which individual servings are taken.

1½ medium onions, sliced into thin rounds
juice of 2 limes
1 tsp hot red pepper sauce

Marinate the onions in the lime juice and red pepper sauce while the rice and beans are cooking.

2 cups brown rice
2 cups water
2 cups tomato juice
1 bay leaf

Simmer the rice, water, tomato juice, and bay leaf together in a tightly covered pot for 35-40 minutes until the rice is tender. Leave the lid on after the heat is turned off to allow the rice to finish cooking. While the rice is cooking, prepare the black beans.

1 onion, chopped
3 cloves garlic, minced
2-3 jalapeño peppers, minced
1 tsp olive oil

In a soup pot, sauté the onion, garlic, and jalapeño peppers in the olive oil until soft.

2 cups tomatoes, chopped
5 cups cooked black beans

Add the tomatoes and black beans to the pot, and simmer while the rice is cooking.

2-3 quarts fresh kale, chopped

Steam the kale until tender.
To serve, put a flat mound of rice in the center of a large platter. Scoop the black bean sauce over the rice. Arrange the cooked kale around the rice. Spread the onion rings over all, and pour the lime marinade over the entire platter.

Per serving: Calories: 413, Protein: 16 gm., Fat: 2 gm., Carbohydrates: 81 gm.

Lima Combo over Couscous

Serves 6

This colorful dish is quick to prepare and has an unusual flavor.

1 cup onions, chopped.
1 bell pepper, chopped
1 cup carrots, diced
1 tsp olive oil

In a large skillet, sauté the onions, bell pepper, and carrots in the olive oil until soft.

2 cups tomatoes, chopped
2 cups zucchini, cubed
1 cup peas
2 cups cooked lima beans
1 tsp fennel seeds

Add the tomatoes, zucchini, peas, lima beans, and fennel seeds, cover, and cook for 10 minutes.

1 cup mushrooms, sliced
¼ cup raisins
½ tsp salt
⅛ tsp crushed red chili pepper, dried (optional)

Add the mushrooms, raisins, salt, and chili pepper to the simmering sauce, and cook slowly for 10 more minutes. Meanwhile, prepare the couscous.

1½ cups couscous
3 cups boiling water

Measure the couscous into a medium serving bowl, pour the boiling water over it, and mix well. Cover and let stand for 10 minutes. Uncover and stir to fluff up. Ladle the lima bean sauce over the couscous, and serve.

Per serving: Calories: 285, Protein: 11 gm., Fat: 1 gm., Carbohydrates: 57 gm.

Fruity Beans

Serves 3-4

*This is a good way to incorporate a surplus of apples or pears into the main part of your meal.
Serve this over rice or millet.*

**2 cups cooked white beans (Great
     Northern, navy, limas)
2 cups apples or pears,
     or 1 cup each, chopped
½ cup onions, chopped
½ cup bean liquid or water
½ Tbsp honey
juice of 1 lemon
1½ Tbsp cider vinegar
½ tsp salt**

In a covered, 3-quart pot, cook the beans, fruit, onions, liquid, honey, lemon juice, vinegar, and salt until the fruit has become quite soft (about 20-25) minutes. Stir occasionally. Leave the lid on and let sit until ready to serve.

Per serving: Calories: 275, Protein: 9 gm., Fat: 0 gm., Carbohydrates: 58 gm.

Marinara Lentil Sauce

Serves 6

This sauce is made to serve with pasta. It's also good as a sauce for lasagne.

2 cloves garlic, chopped
1 cup onions, chopped
1 tsp olive oil

In a deep pot, sauté the garlic and onions in the olive oil until the onions are soft.

1¼ cups lentils
3 cups water

Add the lentils and water to the onions and garlic; cover, bring to a boil, and simmer for 30 minutes.

2 cups fresh or canned tomatoes, chopped
1 chili pepper, minced
2 Tbsp fresh basil,
or ½ tsp dried basil
½ tsp dried oregano

Add the tomatoes, chili pepper, basil and oregano to the lentils, and cook 20 minutes until the lentils are soft.

⅓ cup tomato paste
½-1 tsp salt

Add the tomato paste and salt to the pot, mix until dissolved, uncover, and simmer for 15 minutes. Serve over pasta.

Per serving: Calories: 137, Protein: 8 gm., Fat: 1 gm., Carbohydrates: 24 gm.

Diane's Eggplant and Black-Eyed Pea Curry

Serves 4-6

Diane lived in Varanasi for a while and got the feel for Indian spices and cooking. This can either be a side dish or the focus for a meal accompanied by salad and rice.

1 Tbsp canola oil
½ tsp black mustard seeds
2 dried red peppers

In a medium skillet, heat the oil and add the mustard seeds and red peppers; cook until the mustard seeds begin to pop.

1 cup black-eyed peas, soaked over-
night or 1 (10 oz.) package
frozen black-eyed peas
½ tsp salt
¼ tsp turmeric

Add the black-eyed peas, salt, turmeric, and enough water to cover the peas; cover and cook until the peas are tender (frozen peas will cook faster than soaked peas).

2 medium eggplants, cut into small
cubes with skin
1 small onion, chopped
1 tsp fresh gingerroot, minced
¼ cup water

Add the eggplant, onion, gingerroot, and water; cover, and cook over low heat for 15 minutes.

2 Tbsp coriander leaves

Add the coriander leaves just before the heat is turned off. Keep covered and let sit for several minutes before serving.

Per serving: Calories: 170, Protein: 6 gm., Fat: 3 gm., Carbohydrates: 30 gm.

Coccari's Masoor Dal

Serves 6

This spicy curry dish is quick and easy to prepare. Serve with rice and garnish with fresh coriander leaves for that special touch.

2 cups orange lentils (masoor dal)
½ tsp salt
1 clove garlic, minced
½" piece gingerroot, grated
⅛ tsp ground coriander
⅛ tsp cumin
⅛ tsp turmeric
4½ cups water

Add the orange lentils, salt, garlic, gingerroot, and spices to the water. Bring to a boil, lower the heat, and cook until the lentils are very soft, (about 30 minutes).

2 tsp canola oil
2 cloves garlic, minced
1 medium onion, finely chopped
1" piece of gingerroot, grated
1 tsp cumin seeds
¼ tsp turmeric powder
1 tsp coriander, ground
⅛ tsp Garam Masala (see page 108)
1 dried chili pepper, crushed
**   (optional)**

Heat the oil in a small skillet, add the garlic, onion, and gingerroot, and cook until brown, stirring frequently. Add the remaining spices and cook several more minutes. Add this mixture to the cooked dal, and stir well.

1 Tbsp lemon juice

Mix in the lemon juice right before serving. Serve warm.

Per serving: Calories: 148, Protein: 9 gm., Fat: 2 gm., Carbohydrates: 24 gm.

Soybeans in Sweet Sauce

Serves 4

Have a hankering for something sweet but don't feel like making a desert? Try this simple, yet unusual, combination. The molasses gives it a rich flavor.

½ cup bean stock
1 Tbsp cornstarch
3 Tbsp honey
1 Tbsp blackstrap molasses
2 Tbsp soy sauce

Combine the bean stock, cornstarch, honey, molasses, and soy sauce in a medium saucepan, and bring to a boil, stirring occasionally. Reduce the heat and simmer for 5 minutes.

2 cups cooked soybeans

Add the soybeans to the sauce, and heat thoroughly. Let cool slightly and serve over rice or millet.

Per serving: Calories: 196, Protein: 11 gm., Fat: 5 gm., Carbohydrates: 29 gm.

Anasazi Beans in Miso Sauce

Serves 4-5

2 Tbsp sesame seeds

In a small skillet, roast the sesame seeds until they are browned and start to pop, then grind them in the blender until they are powdered.

1 cup bean stock
1 Tbsp honey
2 Tbsp dark miso
2 cloves garlic, minced

In a medium saucepan, combine the stock, honey, miso, and garlic. Bring to a simmer and stir until the miso blends into the stock.

3 cups cooked anasazi beans

Add the cooked beans and ground sesame seeds to the sauce, and cook for 5-10 minutes. Serve over rice or millet.

Per serving: Calories: 189, Protein: 9 gm., Fat: 2 gm., Carbohydrates: 33 gm.

Spanish Yellow Split Peas

Serves 4-6

2 cups dried yellow split peas
6 cups water

1 tsp olive oil
1 cup carrots, diced
1 cup onions, chopped
3 cloves garlic, minced
1 green pepper, chopped

2 cups canned or fresh tomatoes
¼ cup red wine vinegar
2 tsp chili powder
2 tsp cumin
1 tsp oregano
½ tsp salt

Cook the yellow split peas in the water for about 1½ hours until soft. Soaking the peas first will reduce the cooking time.

While the split peas are cooking, put the olive oil in a large skillet, and sauté the carrots, onions, garlic, and green pepper, for 5 minutes, while stirring.

Add the tomatoes, vinegar, chili powder, cumin, oregano, and salt to the sautéed vegetables; cover and cook for 10 minutes, stirring occasionally. Turn off the heat. When the yellow split peas are soft, transfer them with a slotted spoon to the skillet of vegetables and spices, and cook over medium heat for 15 minutes. Serve with rice or a chunk of whole grain bread.

Per serving: Calories: 142, Protein: 7 gm., Fat: 1 gm., Carbohydrates: 26 gm.

Split Pea Curry

Serves 4-6

2 cups dried green split peas (1 lb.)
6 cups water

Bring the peas to a boil, lower the heat to a simmer, and cook for about 45 minutes. The peas should be tender but still hold their shape. Stir several times and keep the pot partially covered (a tightly covered pot of split peas will boil over).

1 Tbsp garlic, minced
1 Tbsp gingerroot, grated
1 tsp olive oil

In a medium skillet, sauté the garlic and gingerroot in the olive oil for a few minutes being careful not to let the garlic burn.

1 tsp brown mustard seed
1 tsp cumin seeds
1 tsp Garam Masala (see page 108)
½ tsp salt (optional)

Add the mustard and cumin seeds to the garlic and gingerroot, and stir while the seeds pop. Add the garam masala and salt, spoon the cooked split peas into the skillet with the spices, and simmer for 5 minutes or longer. The peas should be thick. Serve over rice.

Per serving: Calories: 199, Protein: 11 gm., Fat: 1 gm., Carbohydrates: 35 gm.

Butternut Aduki Skillet

Serves 5

2 Tbsp fresh garlic, minced
1 tsp olive oil
3 cups butternut squash, peeled and
**   cubed**
⅓ cup water

In a medium skillet, sauté the garlic in the olive oil for 2 minutes. Push the garlic to the side of the skillet, and add the butternut squash to the pan. Pour the water over the squash, cover, and cook for 5-7 minutes until the squash is soft but still firm.

2 cups cooked aduki beans
¼ cup cilantro, chopped

Add the aduki beans and cilantro to the skillet, stir, and cook over medium heat for a few minutes until the beans are heated. Cover, turn off the heat, and let sit for several minutes to allow the flavors to blend.

Per serving: Calories: 175, Protein: 7 gm., Fat: 1 gm., Carbohydrates: 35 gm.

Orange-Ginger Garbanzos

Serves 4-6

1 cup orange juice, fresh squeezed
2 Tbsp tahini
1 Tbsp gingerroot, grated
2 Tbsp soy sauce
1 Tbsp cornstarch

4 cups cooked garbanzo beans

In a medium saucepan, combine the orange juice, tahini, gingerroot, soy sauce, and cornstarch, and whisk or stir well until no lumps are left. Heat over medium heat until the sauce begins to boil, and cook for 1 minute at a gentle boil.

Add the garbanzo beans to the orange sauce mixture, and cook on low heat until the beans are thoroughly heated, about 3 minutes. Cover and turn off heat. Serve over rice.

Per serving: Calories: 285, Protein: 12 gm., Fat: 6 gm., Carbohydrates: 45 gm.

Caribbean Black-Eyed Pea Stir-Fry

Serves 6-8

1½ cups onions, chopped
1 green pepper, chopped
1 cup celery, diced
1 cup carrots, chopped
¾ cup raw cashews
1 cup fresh or frozen green peas
1 tsp olive oil

In a large skillet, sauté the onions, pepper, celery, carrots, cashews, and peas in the olive oil for 3-5 minutes, while stirring.

1 cup pineapple tidbits
¼ cup pineapple juice
2 Tbsp soy sauce
2 cups cooked brown rice
3 cups cooked black-eyed peas

Add the pineapple, pineapple juice, soy sauce, rice, and black-eyed peas to the skillet. Simmer for several minutes while mixing well, and serve hot.

Per serving: Calories: 321, Protein: 11 gm., Fat: 9 gm., Carbohydrates: 50 gm.

East Indian Kidneys

Serves 4

1 cup onions, chopped
1 chili pepper, minced
2 large cloves garlic, minced
1 Tbsp gingerroot, minced or grated
1 tsp olive oil

In a medium skillet, sauté the onions, chili pepper, garlic, and gingerroot in the olive oil, stirring frequently.

2 tsp Garam Masala, (see page 108)
1 Tbsp coriander
1 tsp turmeric
1 tsp cumin, ground
1 cup tomatoes, chopped or pureed

Add the garam masala, coriander, turmeric, cumin, and tomatoes to the skillet, and cook for 5 minutes.

2½ cups cooked kidney beans
1 cup bean stock
½ cup soy yogurt (optional)

Add the kidney beans and stock, bring to a low boil, and simmer for 10 minutes, stirring occasionally. Serve over rice with a spoonful of soy yogurt for topping if desired.

Per serving: Calories: 194, Protein: 9 gm., Fat: 2 gm., Carbohydrates: 35 gm.

Anasazi Beans and Rice

Serves 4-6

What an easy recipe, you say? True, but taste these pretty beans, and you'll see why they don't need a lot of extra flavorings. It's also a good dish to set out with your favorite chutney or relish.

1 cup anasazi beans
4 cups water

Soak the beans in the water overnight. If you're short on time, bring the beans and water to a boil and simmer for 1 minute. Cover and set aside to soak for 1 hour.

1 bay leaf

After the beans have plumped up, drain off the water, add 3 cups of fresh water and the bay leaf, and bring to a boil for 10 minutes.

1 cup brown rice
1 clove garlic, chopped coarsely
1 jalapeño pepper, chopped
1 Tbsp soy sauce

Add the brown rice, garlic, jalapeño pepper, and soy sauce to the boiling beans. Cover, lower the heat to a simmer, and cook gently for 40 minutes.

Per serving: Calories: 235, Protein: 9 gm., Fat: 0 gm., Carbohydrates: 47 gm.

Lentils and Rice

Serves 6

Lentils and rice go together so naturally . . . both chewy and hearty. This dish is very easy to prepare. It lets you concentrate on putting together a fresh tossed salad to accompany your meal.

2 cups lentils
1 cup brown rice
6 cups water

In a tightly covered 3-quart pan, bring the lentils, brown rice, and water to a boil, lower the heat, and simmer for 40 minutes.

1 cup onions, chopped
2 cloves garlic, minced
1 tsp oil

Sauté the onions and garlic in the oil for several minutes until the onions are soft and transparent.

1 tsp cumin
1 tsp coriander
¼ tsp black pepper
1 Tbsp soy sauce

Add the cumin, coriander, black pepper, soy sauce, onions, and garlic to the cooked lentils and rice. Cook for 10 minutes, remove from the heat, and let sit for several minutes.

juice of 1 lemon

Drizzle the lemon juice over each portion before serving.

Per serving: Calories: 268, Protein: 13 gm., Fat: 1 gm., Carbohydrates: 50 gm.

Hoppin' John

Serves 6

This dish is traditionally served with corn bread on New Year's Day to insure good health and prosperity for the year ahead. There is no need to enjoy it only once a year.

1 cup soaked black-eyed peas
⅔ cup uncooked brown rice
1 tsp dried chili pepper
½ cup dried tomatoes
4 cups vegetable broth or water

In a soup pot, add the black-eyed peas, rice, chili pepper, dried tomatoes, and water or broth. Bring to a boil, cover, and simmer for 45 minutes.

5 cloves garlic, minced
1 onion, chopped
½ tsp oil

Sauté the garlic and onion in the oil until soft, and add to the peas and rice when they are done.

2 Tbsp red wine vinegar
½ cup fresh parsley, chopped
salt to taste

Add the vinegar, parsley, and salt to the pot and simmer, uncovered, for 5 minutes.

Per serving: Calories: 165, Protein: 6 gm., Fat: 0 gm., Carbohydrates: 32 gm.

White Bean Tzimmis

Serves 6

Tzimmes is a Jewish dish which is traditionally prepared for the Passover meal. This variation is good any time of year.

1 cup dried white beans
5 cups water

½ cup uncooked brown rice
2 cups carrots, cut into 1" chunks
2 cups sweet potatoes,
**   cut into 1" cubes**
1 cup pitted prunes, halved
1 cup onions, chopped

2 Tbsp honey
juice of 1 lemon
½ tsp salt

Place the beans and water in a 3-quart pot, cover, and cook for 30 minutes.

Add the rice, carrots, sweet potatoes, prunes, and onions, cover, and continue to simmer for 30 minutes.

Add the honey, lemon juice, and salt, and cook for 15-20 minutes until everything is soft and the tzimmis is thick.

Per serving: Calories: 344, Protein: 9 gm., Fat: 0 gm., Carbohydrates: 74 gm.

Spicy Anasazi Beans

Serves 4

1 cup anasazi beans
4 cups water

2 cloves garlic, minced
1 cup onions, chopped
¾ cup bell peppers, chopped
2 chili peppers, minced
1 tsp olive oil

2 cups tomatoes, chopped
2 Tbsp tomato paste
1 tsp cumin
1 tsp coriander
1 tsp paprika
1 tsp turmeric
½ tsp salt

Soak the beans overnight; drain, rinse, and add 4 cups of fresh water. Bring to a boil, cover, and cook until soft (about 1 hour).

In a medium skillet, sauté the garlic, onions, and peppers in the olive oil, stirring frequently to prevent sticking. Cook until the onions and peppers are soft.

Add the tomatoes, tomato paste, spices, and anasazi beans to the skillet, and cook for 10 minutes. Serve over rice.

Per serving: Calories: 199, Protein: 9 gm., Fat: 0 gm., Carbohydrates: 38 gm.

Black Beans and Noodles

Serves 6

**2 cups uncooked whole wheat pasta
(½ lb.)**

Cook the pasta in lightly salted boiling water until al dente. Drain, rinse, and set aside.

**2 cloves garlic, minced
4-5 scallions, chopped
2½ cups cabbage, shredded
1 cup celery, chopped
1 tsp canola oil
¼ cup soy sauce
1 Tbsp cilantro, minced**

In a large skillet, sauté the garlic, scallions, cabbage, and celery in the canola oil for 5 minutes until soft. Stir in the soy sauce and cilantro while the vegetables are cooking.

2½ cups cooked black beans

Add the pasta and beans to the vegetables, and heat while mixing well. Cover and simmer for a few minutes to blend the flavors, and serve hot.

Per serving: Calories: 288, Protein: 14 gm., Fat: 2 gm., Carbohydrates: 53 gm.

Pasta Fagioli

Serves 4-5

This easy-to-prepare dish is a favorite with the kids and good any time of year.

½ cup onions, chopped
1 cup carrots, diced
½ cup celery, chopped
1 tsp olive oil

In a large skillet, sauté the onions, carrots, and celery in the olive oil for 5 minutes.

1 cup fresh or canned tomatoes,
chopped
1 tsp garlic powder
½ tsp salt
¼ tsp black pepper

Add the tomatoes, garlic powder, salt, and black pepper to the skillet, and cook 5 more minutes.

2 cups cooked white beans (Great
Northern or cannellini)
4 cups cooked small shells
or elbow macaroni

Mix in the white beans and pasta, cover, and cook on low heat until thoroughly heated.

Per serving: Calories: 291, Protein: 12 gm., Fat: 1 gm., Carbohydrates: 56 gm.

Bean Balls with Mushroom Gravy

Serves 6

½ cup wheat germ
1 cup whole wheat bread crumbs
½ cup soymilk

3 cups cooked navy beans
1 small onion, minced
¼ tsp coriander
½ tsp salt

Mushroom Gravy:
1 cup mushrooms, chopped

1½ cups soymilk,
    or ¾ cup soymilk + ¾ cup
    water
3 Tbsp cornstarch
2 Tbsp soy sauce
¼ tsp garlic powder

Combine the wheat germ, bread crumbs, and soymilk in a bowl. Let sit to allow the soymilk to be absorbed by the bread crumbs while you prepare the beans.

Mash the beans or mix in a food processor, and add the onion, coriander, and salt. Squeeze any excess liquid from the soaking bread crumbs (set the liquid aside for the gravy), and combine the bread crumbs with bean mixture. Mix thoroughly and shape into 1" balls. Place the balls side by side in a vegetable steamer (they'll expand a little bit), cover, and steam for 10 minutes. After they are steamed, turn off the heat, keep covered, and let sit 5 minutes before serving.

In a saucepan, cook the mushrooms in a few spoonfuls of water long enough to soften.

Combine the soymilk and cornstarch first, then add to the mushrooms while stirring with a wire whisk to avoid lumps. Add the soy sauce and garlic powder, and continue to whisk until the sauce thickens and begins to bubble. Serve over the bean balls.

Per serving: Calories: 255, Protein: 14 gm., Fat: 4 gm., Carbohydrates: 42 gm.

Succotash

Serves 5-6

When I was a child, we enjoyed this dish when the lima beans were fresh from the garden. It's also good using dried lima beans.

1 onion, chopped
1 clove garlic, minced
¾ cup celery, chopped
1 tsp olive oil

In a large skillet, sauté the onion, garlic, and celery in the olive oil until the onion and celery are soft.

3 Tbsp flour
1 Tbsp soy sauce
1 cup water or bean broth

Stir the flour, soy sauce, and water or broth together in a small bowl. Pour over the onion, garlic, and celery mixture, whisking until a smooth sauce is formed.

Preheat the oven to 350°.

2 cups cooked lima beans
2½ cups corn, fresh or frozen
⅔ cup soymilk
⅛ tsp nutmeg

Add the lima beans, corn, soymilk, and nutmeg to the skillet, and heat up just to boiling. Pour into an oiled casserole dish, and bake for 20-25 minutes.

Per serving: Calories: 385, Protein: 14 gm., Fat: 2 gm., Carbohydrates: 77 gm.

* Desserts *

Tutti-Fruity Bars

Yields 20 pieces

This is a chewy fruit bar that is good for breakfast or as a snack. It keeps well in the refrigerator.

2 Tbsp canola oil
1 ripe banana
¾ cup applesauce
1 cup cooked soybeans
¾ cup figs
½ cup orange juice
1 tsp vanilla
⅓ cup honey

3 cups unbleached white flour
¼ tsp salt
1 tsp baking soda
1 tsp baking powder

In a food processor, combine the canola oil, banana, applesauce, soybeans, figs, orange juice, vanilla, and honey, and process until smooth. The figs will stay chunky. Pour into a mixing bowl.

Preheat the oven to 350°.

Sift the flour, salt, baking soda, and baking powder into the mixing bowl, and stir into the wet mixture. Pour into a lightly oiled 9" x 13" pan, and bake for 25 minutes. Cut into pieces when cool.

Per piece: Calories: 139, Protein: 3 gm., Fat: 2 gm., Carbohydrates: 26 gm.

Aduki Carob Cake

Yields 9 pieces

¾ cup honey
3 Tbsp canola oil
1 cup cooked aduki beans
½ cup soymilk
1 tsp vanilla

Combine the honey, canola oil, aduki beans, soymilk, and vanilla in a food processor. Blend together until smooth, and pour into a mixing bowl.

1½ cups flour
½ cup carob powder
1 tsp baking soda
¼ tsp salt

Sift the flour, carob powder, baking soda, and salt into the bowl of blended liquid ingredients. Beat or whisk them together until a smooth batter is formed. Pour into a lightly oiled, 9" square cake pan, and bake for 25 minutes.

Per piece: Calories: 255, Protein: 4 gm., Fat: 5 gm., Carbohydrates: 49 gm.

Sweet Bean Pie

Serves 8   (one 9" pie)

From San Francisco to New York, these pies are sold as little tarts by Muslim street vendors.

Crust:
½ cup whole wheat flour
½ cup unbleached white flour
⅛ tsp salt
1 tsp sesame seeds
2 Tbsp canola oil (the more oil
you use, the less chewy and
more flaky the crust will be)
⅓ cup water

Mix the flours, salt, sesame seeds, canola oil, and water with a fork. Work the dough with your hands until a smooth ball forms. Add more water if the dough is too dry or tends to break when you are rolling it out. Add more flour if the dough is too sticky. On a floured board, roll out the dough into a circle about 13" in diameter. Move the crust into a 9" pie pan, turn the outer edge under, and press it with a fork or make a fluted design with your fingers. Put the crust aside until the filling is ready.

Preheat the oven to 350°.

Filling:
1⅓ cups low-fat soymilk
3 cups cooked white beans
⅔ cup honey
½ tsp vanilla
1 tsp cinnamon
¼ tsp cloves
½ tsp ground ginger
⅛ tsp salt
2 Tbsp unbleached white flour

Put the soymilk, white beans, honey, vanilla, cinnamon, cloves, ginger, salt, and flour in a blender, and combine until creamy. Pour into the unbaked pie shell, and bake for 45 minutes. Cool before serving.

Per serving: Calories: 278, Protein: 8 gm., Fat: 4 gm., Carbohydrates: 51 gm.

Index

A

aduki beans
  Butternut Aduki Skillet   125
Aduki Carob Cake   139
African Split Pea Soup   41
alpha-galactosidase   8
anasazi beans
  Spicy Anasazi Beans   133
Anasazi Beans and Rice   129
Anasazi Beans in Miso Sauce   122
Armenian Beans   110
Autumn Stew   89
Autumn White Bean Soup   40

B

Baked Beans, Pat's   60
Barbecue Black Bean Dip   20
Barbecue Soybeans   100
Bean
  Balls with Mushroom Gravy   136
  Sausage Links   81
  Sprout Curry   107
bean cooking chart   11
Beano   9
beans, types of   12
Black Bean Soup   45
black beans
  Barbecue Black Bean Dip   20
  Brazilian Black Beans   115
  Tamale Stuffed Peppers   77
  Tropical Black Bean Salad   29
Black Beans and Noodles   134
Black Eyed Peas with Greens   114
Black Eyed Spirals   78
black-eyed peas
  Caribbean Black-Eyed Pea Stir-
    Fry   127
  Diane's Eggplant and Black-Eyed
    Pea Curry   119
  Hoppin' John   131
  Stuffed Cabbage with Black-eyed
    Peas   74
Brazilian Black Beans   115
Butternut Aduki Skillet   125

C

Caribbean Black-Eyed Pea Stir-
  Fry   127
Carrot and Garbanzo Salad   25
Carrot-Garbanzo Dip   22
casseroles
  Noodle-Veggie-Bean Casse-
    role   61
  Spicy Pinto Casserole   64
Ceci all' Italiana   113
Chick-Pea Nuts   24
Coccari's Masoor Dal   120
Composite Soup   56
cooking beans   9
cooking chart, bean   11
Creamy Corn Soup   53
Creamy Pinto Soup   46
Crunchy Soybean Salad   36
Curried
  Garbanzos   106
  Limas   111
  Veggie Fritters   88

D

DARK STAR Dip   16
Desserts
  Aduki Carob Cake   139
  Sweet Bean Pie   140
  Tutti-Fruity Bars   138
Diane's Eggplant and Black-Eyed Pea
  Curry   119
dip
  Barbecue Black Bean Dip   20
  Carrot-Garbanzo Dip   22
DARK STAR Dip   16
Golden Yellow Split Pea Dip   23
West Indies Bean Dip   19

E

East Indian Kidneys   128
Easy White Bean Stew   97
Eggplant rolls   80
Enchiladas   66

F

Falafel   82
freezing beans   10
Fruity Beans   117

G

galactosemic   9
Garam Masala   108
garbanzo beans
  Carrot and Garbanzo Salad   25
  Carrot-Garbanzo Dip   22
  Ceci all' Italiana   113
  Curried Garbanzos   106
  Falafel   82
  Garbanzo Gumbo   105
  Garbanzo Spread   17
  Garbanzo Sweet Potato Stew   96
  Garbanzo-Vegetable Loaf   71
  Hummus   18
  Moussaka   62
  Olive Pasta Salad   38
  Orange Ginger Garbanzos   126
  Spanish Stew   91
  Stuffed Acorn Squash   73
  Sweet 'n Sour Garbanzo
    Medley   99
  Tabouli   27
Golden Yellow Split Pea Dip   23
Great Northern Mushroom
  Soup   42
Gremalata   16

H

Hearty Bean 'n Grain Soup   49
Hoppin' John   131
Hummus   18

I

Island Loaf   72

K

Karhi and Pakoris (Dumplings)   58
kidney beans
    East Indian Kidneys   128
    Kidney Bean and Sprouted Lentil
        Salad   28
    Kidney Bean Salad   33
    Kidney-Polenta Stew   93
    Kidney-Yam Stew   95
    Sweet 'n Sour Cabbage-Kidney
        Salad   39
    Tanzanian Kidneys with Coco-
        nut   102

L

lentils
    Coccari's Masoor Dal   120
    Hearty Bean 'n Grain Soup   49
    Lentil Burgers   84
    Lentil Loaf   70
    Lentil Paté   21
    Lentil Soup with Greens   51
    Lentil Stew   94
    Lentil-Lime Salad   31
    Lentils and Eggplant   101
    Lentils and Rice   130
    Lentils 'n Barley   98
    Lentil-Vegetable Biryani   90
    Pineapple-Lentil Salad   32
    Spicy Lentils   103

lima beans
    American Beans   110
    Autumn Stew   89
    Composite Soup   56
    Creamy Corn Soup   53
    Curried Limas   111
    Lima Combo over Cous-
        cous   116
    Lima Gazpacho Salad   26
    Succotash   137
    Triple Bean Soup   52
loaf
    Garbanzo-Vegetable Loaf   *71*
    Island Loaf   72
    Lentil Loaf   70

M

Marinara Lentil Sauce   118
Meatless Pinto Balls   87
Melted Yeast Cheeze Sauce   65
Mexican Corn Bean Pie   68
Mixed Bean and Noodle Soup   44
Moussaka   62

N

navy beans
    Bean Balls with Mushroom
        Gravy   136
    Island Loaf   72
    Pat's Baked Beans   60
    Triple Bean Soup   52
Noodle-Veggie-Bean Casserole   61

O

Olive Pasta Salad   38
Orange-Ginger Garbanzos   126

P

Pasta Bean Salad   35
Pasta Fagioli   135

Pasta Plus Soup   47
Pat's Baked Beans   60
Pineapple-Lentil Salad   32
pinto beans
    Creamy Pinto Soup   46
    Curried Veggie Fritters   88
    DARK STAR Dip   16
    Eggplant Rolls   80
    Enchiladas   66
    Meatless Pinto Balls   87
    Mexican Corn Bean Pie   68
    Pasta Bean Salad   35
    Pasta Plus Soup   47
    Pinto Burgers   83
    Pinto Pies   86
    Spicy Pinto Casserole   64
    Taco Salad   30
    Triple Bean Soup   52
    West Indies Bean Dip   19
preparing beans   10

S

salad
    Carrot and Garbanzo Salad   25
    Crunchy Soybean Salad   36
    Kidney Bean and Sprouted Lentil
        Salad   28
    Kidney Bean Salad   33
    Lentil-Lime Salad   31
    Lima Gazpacho Salad   26
    Olive Pasta Salad   38
    Pasta Bean Salad   35
    Pineapple-Lentil Salad   32
    Sweet 'n Sour Cabbage-Kidney
        Salad   39
    Tabouli   27
    Taco Salad   30
    Thai Style Bean Salad   37
    Tropical Black Bean Salad   29
    White Bean Salad   34

Sauce, Melted Yeast Cheeze   65
soup
   African Split Pea Soup   41
   Autumn White Bean Soup   40
   Black Bean Soup   45
   Composite Soup   56
   Creamy Corn Soup   53
   Creamy Pinto Soup   46
   Great Northern Mushroom
      Soup   42
   Hearty Bean 'n Grain Soup   49
   Lentil, with Greens Soup   51
   Mixed Bean and Noodle
      Soup   44
   Pasta Plus Soup   47
   Spicy Golden Soup   55
   Split Pea Soup   54
   Sprouted Lentil Soup   48
   Summer Minestrone Soup   50
   Triple Bean Soup   52
   Yellow Split Pea Soup   43
soybeans
   Barbecue Soybeans   100
   Bean Sausage Links   81
   Crunchy Soybean Salad   36
   Noodle-Veggie-Bean Casse-
      role   61
   Soy Burgers   85
   Soy Nuts   24
   Soy Stuffed Peppers   76
   Soybean Stroganoff   109
   Soybeans in Sweet Sauce   121
   Sweet and Sour Soybeans   104
   Tutti-Fruity Bars   138
Spanish Stew   91
Spanish Yellow Split Peas   123
Spicy
   Anasazi Beans   133
   Golden Soup   55
   Lentils   103
   Pinto Casserole   64
Split Pea Curry   124
Split Pea Soup   54

split peas
   African Split Pea Soup   41
   Autumn Stew   89
   Composite Soup   56
   Golden Yellow Split Pea Dip   23
   Hearty Bean 'n Grain Soup   49
   Spanish Yellow Split Peas   123
   Spicy Golden Soup   55
   Yellow Split Pea Soup   43
Sprouted Lentil Soup   48
Sprouted Lentils   108
Stuffed Acorn Squash   73
Stuffed Cabbage with Black-Eyed
      Peas   74
Succotash   137
Summer Lentils and Veggies   112
Summer Minestrone Soup   50
Sweet and Sour Soybeans   104
Sweet Bean Pie   140
Sweet 'n Sour Cabbage-Kidney
      Salad   39
Sweet 'n Sour Garbanzo Medley   99

T

Tabouli   27
Taco Salad   30
Tamale Stuffed Peppers   77
Tanzanian Kidneys with Coco-
      nut   102
Thai Style Bean Salad   37
Triple Bean Soup   52
Tropical Black Bean Salad   29
Tutti-Fruity Bars   138
types of beans   12

W

West Indies Bean Dip   19
White Bean
   and Squash Stew   92
   Chowder   57
   Salad   34
   Spread   15
   Tzimmis   132

white beans
   Autumn White Bean Soup   40
   Easy White Bean Stew   97
   Fruity Beans   117
   Gremalata   16
   Karhi and Pakoris   58
   Mixed Bean and Noodle
      Soup   44
   Pasta Fagioli   135
   Summer Minestrone Soup   50
   Sweet Bean Pie   140
   Thai Style Bean Salad   37

Y

Yellow Split Pea Soup   43

Ask your store to carry these books, or you may order directly from:

The Book Publishing Company
P.O. Box 99
Summertown, TN 38483

Or call: 1-800-695-2241
Please add $2.00 per book for shipping

American Harvest	$11.95
Regional Recipes for the Vegetarian Kitchen	
Burgers 'n Fries 'n Cinnamon Buns	$ 6.95
Cooking with Gluten and Seitan	$ 7.95
Ecological Cooking: Recipes to Save the Planet	$10.95
From A Traditional Greek Kitchen	$ 9.95
George Bernard Shaw Vegetarian Cookbook	$ 8.95
Instead of Chicken, Instead of Turkey:	$ 9.95
A Poultryless "Poultry" Potpourri	
Judy Brown's Guide to Natural Foods Cooking	$10.95
Kids Can Cook	$ 9.95
Murrieta Hot Springs Vegetarian Cookbook	$ 9.95
The Now & Zen Epicure	
Gourmet Cuisine for the Enlightened Palate	$17.95
The New Farm Vegetarian Cookbook	$ 8.95
The Peaceful Cook	$ 8.95
A Physician's Slimming Guide, Neal D. Barnard, M..D.	$ 5.95
Also by Dr. Barnard:	
The Power of Your Plate	$11.95
Live Longer, Live Better (90 min. cassette)	$ 9.95
Beyond Animal Experiments (90 min. cassette)	$ 9.95
The Shoshoni Cookbook	$12.95
Soups For All Seasons	$ 9.95
The Sprout Garden:	$ 8.95
Indoor Growers Guide to Gourmet Sprouts	
Starting Over: Learning to Cook with Natural Foods	$10.95
The Tempeh Cookbook	$10.95
Ten Talents (Vegetarian Cookbook)	$18.95
Tofu Cookery	$14.95
Tofu Quick & Easy	$ 7.95
The TVP Cookbook	$ 6.95
The Uncheese Cookbook	$11.95
Uprisings: The Whole Grain Bakers' Book	$13.95
Vegetarian Cooking for People with Diabetes	$10.95